THE

NG

SPLASHDOWN

1.

GW01607582

Jay's powered glide carried her into a good lead from the moment she broke the surface. Her rhythm was quickly established and she had the adrenalin of competition flowing through her body.

It took Tally half a length of the pool to develop any sort of fluency in her arm and leg movements. There was a lot to remember. Jay's flying start had unnerved rather than irritated her. It made her think that she was slow and disorganized and she didn't like that. It felt good to compete, and she suddenly knew she had the will to win.

Also in THE SWIMMING CLUB series:

Book 2: Jump In

THE SWIMMING CLUB

SPLASHDOWN

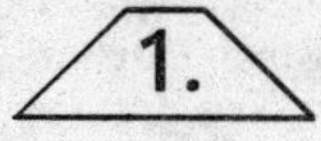

Michael Hardcastle

Hippo Books
Scholastic Publications Limited
London

Scholastic Publications Ltd.,
10 Earlham Street, London WC2H 9RX, UK

Scholastic Inc.,
730 Broadway, New York, NY 10003, USA

Scholastic Tab Publications Ltd.,
123 Newkirk Road, Richmond Hill,
Ontario L4C 3G5, Canada

Ashton Scholastic Pty. Ltd.,
P O Box 579, Gosford, New South Wales,
Australia

Ashton Scholastic Ltd.,
165 Marua Road, Panmure, Auckland 6,
New Zealand

First published by
Scholastic Publications Ltd., 1989

Text copyright © Michael Hardcastle, 1989

Illustration copyright © Jean Foster, 1989

ISBN 0 590 76032 7

All rights reserved
Made and printed by Cox and Wyman Ltd., 1989

Typeset in Times by COLLAGE (Design in Print),
Longfield Hill, Kent.

This book is sold subject to the condition that it shall not, by way of trade or otherwise be lent, resold, hired out, or otherwise circulated without the publisher's prior consent in any form of binding or cover other than that in which it is published and without a similar condition, including this condition, being imposed upon the subsequent purchaser.

CONTENTS

1. Hidden Depths 7
2. Going Places 22
3. Solo Swim 38
4. Urge to Compete 52
5. Conkered! 68
6. 'A Bit Rapid' 83
7. The Real Race 95

HIDDEN DEPTHS

Panic set in after several seconds. Tally, who'd been watching the water with only casual interest, hurried to the edge. Why hadn't Hughie come to the surface? Nobody could remain under much longer — and stay alive.

But still there was no sign of him. The ripples at the point where he'd gone under had disappeared. No one could tell from the appearance of the river that somebody was in there. It looked normal: frighteningly normal.

"Come on, come on, get out!" she yelled, finding her voice at last. Her hands went up to tug at her hair behind her neck, a gesture she always made whenever she was worried about anything. *"Please!"* she added, in a silent plea.

Then, as she tried to make up her mind what to do, a sudden movement to her right caught her eye. Astonished, she saw a girl of about her own age stripping off her jeans and T-shirt, revealing a very colourful swimming costume. Oblivious, apparently, of Tally's presence, she raised herself on her toes on the towpath and then dived head first into the river as if from a springboard. In spite of her own worries about the submerged boy it registered with Tally that this girl with the short, highlighted hair moved as gracefully as a dancer. But where had she come from? And had she really dived in to save the boy while she, Tally, hesitated?

She moved smoothly through the calm water, heading effortlessly for the spot where Hughie had vanished. There was no doubt in Tally's mind about her intentions now. Yet to react so swiftly must mean that she had been watching them and seen Hughie's stupidity. So what else had she seen before Hughie jumped in?

Suddenly, Hughie's head and shoulders came out of the water — but much further downstream than Tally would have believed possible. After all, the current was barely discernible. With a cheery wave in her direction he signalled his well being — and then slipped into a lazy-looking backstroke. At that point he was still unaware of the presence of the girl swimming to save him. She, too, was surprised. She hadn't expected him to resurface so far from the point where he'd gone down. Now she was still several metres away from him. That hardly mattered, though, for it was plain he didn't need her help. His spell underwater seemed not to have affected him at all.

"There's somebody swimming out to get you!" Tally yelled, more to vent her annoyance than to alert Hughie to the presence of another swimmer. She had the satisfaction of seeing his startled look. It didn't take him long to locate the girl in the rainbow costume, who was also looking distinctly annoyed; she could tell that the boy was all right but she still felt the need to ask him if everything was O.K.

"Oh, sure!" he sang out; and promptly disappeared underwater again.

She suspected that he might have some submarine games in mind and she was in no mood to be the target of his attack. She'd met enough jokers in the water to last her a lifetime. With a quick turn, she swam back to the bank and hauled herself from the river. "Well, that was a complete waste of time," she announced to Tally, as she shook water from her hair and then slicked more away from her arms and legs with her fingers. Tally had never seen anyone try to dry themselves like that before. She noticed that this girl had exceptionally long fingers for someone of her age, which Tally judged to be about the same as her own.

"Did you know that he was just fooling around; that he could stay under water as long as that?" she demanded as she continued to stroke herself dry.

Tally's hands linked behind her neck again. "No idea. Don't really know him, except that his name's Hughie. He came to live near us, that's all."

"He's not your boyfriend then?" asked the girl, her eyes narrowing with suspicion.

"Course not!" Tally knew she was colouring up

but she couldn't stop it. "Don't like boys all that much, and certainly not him. He's a great show off, I reckon."

"But when I first saw you both I thought he was kissing you," the questioner persisted.

"No, he just said he could show me he could give the kiss of life to anybody who might have drowned — or nearly drowned." So they *had* been seen after all. Tally was annoyed. She didn't like anyone to have an advantage over her. "I told him I wasn't going to drown. But Hughie — that's his name: pretty deadly, isn't it? — Hughie's the sort who won't give up if he thinks he can get what he wants. *You* know."

The other girl now reached into a sports bag that had been hidden under her discarded clothes and which Tally hadn't even noticed. She took out a pink towel and briskly finished the drying operation before running a comb through her hair. Tally couldn't help being impressed by her obvious organization.

"What's your name then?" the girl asked, unexpectedly.

"Tally." Then, before the next question could be framed, she asked her own. "And what's yours?"

"Jay."

"What — like the bird?"

"If you like," Jay replied,with a shrug of one bare shoulder. Although the sun had gone in and it was distinctly cooler than half-an-hour earlier she seemed to be in no hurry to get dressed again. But her attention was on Hughie, now visible and performing some aquatic gymnastics that involved going round and round in circles. She knew he wanted her to watch him — wanted both of them to — but she found she couldn't resist for the moment.

"Is it short for anything? You know, it sounds, well, just like an initial, not a proper name."

"No, it's my proper name," Jay told her positively. "What about yours? Short for Natalie, is it?"

Tally sighed, reluctant to go through the explanation she'd already had to give so many times. But she'd discovered there was no real alternative. "No, it's actually Tallahassee. And before you go on about it, yes, I know it's a crazy name but my mum chose it because she was once in love with some American folk singer who lived in Tallahassee — that's in Florida — and she couldn't get over what a terrific name it is. Well *she* thinks it is."

"What's your dad think?"

"He thinks it's terrific, too; that's the crazy thing. So that's why I got saddled with it. Dad says Mum loves him now and has forgotten all about her magical folk singer, who she never met anyway."

"Do you like it?" Jay had now managed to divert her attention from Hughie completely and was stepping into her jeans.

"Oh, I've got used to it. I think being called Tally is O.K. I mean, it's different. Bit like yours, I suppose. I don't want to be the same as everybody else. I want to be — myself."

If she'd known Jay as a friend she might have confessed that she wanted to be special. But it was too soon for that. In any case, she wasn't sure she would really like Jay if she got to know her well.

"Can you swim?" was Jay's next question.

"What? Course I can!" Tally was thoroughly indignant. "Can't everybody?"

Jay shook her head. "Course they can't. Otherwise people wouldn't drown, would they? I thought that's why you weren't diving in the river to rescue what's-his-name — Hugh, is it? I mean, if somebody stays under the water as long as he did they usually call out the lifeguards, don't they? They do on the beaches, anyway. So I thought you must have been scared for your own life."

Tally tried to swallow her indignation and conceal the truth: she had been worried, very worried, about Hughie's stupid disappearing act. "I thought he was fooling about but I didn't know for sure," she pointed out. "And I was right, wasn't I?"

"You said before that you didn't know if he was fooling about," Jay said. "But it doesn't matter. Look, are you any good at swimming? I mean, could you win races and that sort of thing?"

"I can beat anybody in my class," Tally responded immediately. Then, a trifle reluctantly, she added, "But nobody bothers much about swimming at our school, not really. I mean, as long as you can swim, keep yourself afloat, that's all that matters. The teachers aren't very geared-up about swimming. But I like it. I'd like to be — well, pretty good, really."

Tally had never admitted that to anyone before and she was surprised to hear herself saying all this. Until that moment she'd hardly recognized her ambitions herself.

Having dried herself off completely, Jay zipped up her sports bag and squatted down on one of the solid wooden benches that lined the towpath, pulling her legs up under her. She was, Tally decided, like no other girl she'd ever met. Jay's dark brown eyes were regarding her speculatively.

"You ought to join The Swimming Club if you want to be good," Jay told her. "Then you could find out how to really improve."

"Which one's that? What's it called?" Tally asked. She would have liked to sit beside Jay but there wasn't much room on the backless bench because of the way Jay was sitting. It was a curious feeling, but it seemed as if Jay was assessing her as a prospective friend or rival. Yet Tally wasn't at all sure that she even liked this girl with the long fingers and the long legs and flattish sort of nose who seemed to have such a superior attitude to life.

"It's called The Swimming Club because it is *the* one — the best there is around," Jay explained. "Janet — she's the coach — she's going—"

"A woman coach? I thought all swimming coaches were men. So—"

"Men don't run everything, you know. Janet's — well, she's a top—"

"Men *should* run everything because they're the greatest!" declared a voice startlingly close to the girls. "Anyway, what're you talking about?"

They both turned to see that Hughie had pulled

himself out of the river and crept up behind them. Arms akimbo, he was standing within a couple of metres of Tally, a huge grin on his broad face.

"Don't you creep up on me, you creep!" Tally showed her irritation; she hadn't forgiven him for fooling her with his underwater disappearance.

The first thing that struck Jay about this spiky-haired boy was the remarkable blue of his eyes: they seemed to glow like sapphires. But there was a warmth in them that real jewels didn't possess.

"Go on, then, what're you on about?" he asked again, this time giving most of his attention to Jay.

"We're talking about The Swimming Club," said Jay, quietly. "Maybe *you* have heard of it?"

"So what's it called?" asked Hughie, predictably.

"That's what it's called, just that," Tally charged in. "Jay here says it doesn't need any other name because it's the greatest."

"Well, I've never heard of it so it can't be that good," Hughie replied. "Anyway, what's special about it."

His arms were now folded across his chest and he was staring challengingly at Jay. She wasn't as pretty as Tally but she looked interesting, all the same.

"It's where, if you're any good at swimming, you'll get better," Jay answered. "We—"

"I *am* good!" Hughie told her, emphatically. "The best you'll ever see at the backstroke. Didn't you see me in the river just now? I can swim for miles underwater without coming up for air. That's how I go so fast."

"I did see," Jay admitted. But that was all she said. She sensed that if she praised him in any way at all his boasting would be boundless.

"She thought you were drowning so she dived in to save your life," Tally told him. "I didn't think you could stay down as long as that."

Although it seemed impossible, Hughie's grin widened a fraction. Then, to demonstrate his prowess, he drew in lungfuls of air. To show that he wasn't cheating in any way as he held his breath he even pinched his nostrils with his left hand. His chest seemed to swell visibly as the girls watched him and colour was rising in his cheeks. Yet he succeeded in keeping it in until until they were sure he was really going to explode with the effort. When, at last, he opened his mouth, the air burst out like a shot from a cannon.

"Not bad," Jay murmured.

"You what?" Hughie demanded, exploding again and revealing just what formidable lung power he did possess. "It's fantastic! Bet you never met anybody who could last as long as that. You never will, neither!"

"Are you good at anything else?" asked Jay, laconically. She was impressed, deeply impressed, but Hughie didn't need any praise from her while he was lavishing so much on himself.

"Best basketball player you'll ever see, no danger. Best player in the whole of Fentown — thats my last school. And it'll be the same at this new school."

"I didn't know there were basketball players of your size," said Jay, assessing his height again."I mean—"

"There's no need to be a giant to be a good basketball player," Hughie told her rather aggressively, his amiable manner falling away like the drops of water from his arms and sturdy legs. "Timing's as important as anything and my timing is spot on. Oh, and I can jump like — like an Olympic high jumper. *That's* what you need: springs in your heels. My best teacher used to say that."

"Anything else you're good at?" Jay continued in a mild tone, sounding genuinely interested rather than amused.

"Running — loads of stamina. Good lungs, you see. Tennis: nobody can last longer than me in rallies even if they've got better shots. Oh, trampoline, too, though I won't get much chance of that here, I suppose. Boy who lived next to me in Fentown had one in his *garden* so I got miles of practice. But not many other people have one, do they?" He paused but he wasn't really waiting for an answer. For the moment he'd run out of "bests" he could claim. Now he stared at the girl sitting so tidily on the bench. "Are you good at anything, then?"

"Asking questions," she replied, solemn faced. It was Tally, against her instincts, who giggled.

"Go on, then, ask me something else," Hughie invited.

"Do you want to join The Swimming Club, the one I've been telling you about?" Jay inquired to his surprise. He'd been sure she would ask him about some of his other accomplishments and he was busily trying to compile a list. Normally, he wasn't keen on club or team events: you were tied down with rules and by having to think about other people's needs. Still, it might be useful to get to know some more people quickly besides Jay herself. Tally didn't seem to be as much fun as he had thought when he first saw her.

"So what's in it for me?" he asked. He was beginning to feel a little chilled after his immersion but he wanted to give Jay a chance to admire his build. Hughie had noticed the sharp glances she was giving him when she thought he wasn't looking at her.

"Isn't that typical of you!" Tally exploded before Jay had a chance to answer. "That's all you think about, getting what *you* want."

"Everybody's the same," Hughie replied, calmly. "What's wrong with it? Anyway, how do *you* know what I'm like? You didn't know I existed until last Monday when me and my family moved into the same road as you. But I know you're a stuck-up thing, that you just curl up if anybody says anything about having a bit of fun. So—"

"That's not true and—"

"Hey, pack it in, you two!" Jay cut in, smiling now for the first time and capturing Hughie's interest once again. "It's fair enough for Hugh to ask what's in it for him. No point in joining something, is there, if you aren't going to get something out of it! Well, I get lots of things out of The Swimming Club and you could, too. Competitions — Janet's terrifically keen on getting people to prove themselves. That's how she puts it. She says if you're winning races it makes you feel good in everything. Janet's a great believer in competition. So we have competitions against other clubs and go on trips to take on the opposition — individual and team events."

"So you get prizes and medals — and other trophies, right?" asked Hughie, his interest level plainly beginning to rise.

"Oh sure, if you're good enough," Jay nodded. "But the competition's pretty hot at The Club. Janet always wants top swimmers as members, not duffers. Oh, and we also get involved in area and county matches, sometimes. That's where the trophies are really something."

"You got any yourself?" Hughie wanted to know.

"Er, one or two," she admitted, but without any intention of elaborating. "Look, why don't you come along tomorrow night and see how you like it? I mean, if you think we're all, well, rubbish, you can just drift off again. Janet won't mind you having a look round — and a free swim." She turned to the girl still frowning at Hughie. "You, too, Tally, if you'd like to."

"Is everything you do in competitions, then?" Tally asked suspiciously.

"Course not! We have lots of fun as well. Lots of games and things — oh, and a crazy tea party in the pool just before Christmas!" Jay paused. "But most of the kids do take winning very seriously, you know. They like winning."

"Sounds great!" Hughie declared, rather to Jay's surprise. He was the one she wanted to see join The Club.She wanted to know what Janet would make of his ability to remain submerged for so long without breathing. It didn't really concern Jay whether Tally came along or not. In any case, Tally might well be simply hopeless in the water.

"So you'll come along and join us — well, see what you think of it?" Jay pressed. "There's some coaching tomorrow night. Janet likes to have regular sessions, you see. Keeps everybody on their toes, she says."

"That's no good in the water, though, is it?" Hughie remarked, somehow managing to keep a smile off his face.

Jay was genuinely puzzled. "I don't get you."

Now Hughie chortled. "And I thought you were the smart one! Look you don't *stand* on your toes in a *swimming* pool, do you?

"Oh, I get you — very funny." Jay smiled graciously, anxious not to disappoint the boy at this stage. "Well, I'm glad you're interested. See you tomorrow night, then? We usually get there about half six, time for a splash around before Janet gets down to serious work."

"I just jump into a cab, then, do I, and tell the driver, 'Take me to The Swimming Club' and he'll know where to go. Right?" said Hughie, grin-less again.

"What? Oh, I see what you mean. Sorry. It's on Rule Street, near the library, almost opposite that new big hotel, the Cavendish or something. There's a silver plate beside the door — it's a red door — and it says that it's for members only. But you just tell anybody who asks you that you've come to join and you'll be O.K. Or you can say that Miss Gainfield — that's Janet — wants to see you."

"I'm not promising, you know," Hughie told her, although he had every intention of being there the following evening. "I mean, something else might come up, something more interesting."

Jay unfolded her legs and stood up, tucking her sports bag under one arm. "Well, that's up to you." She glanced at Tally. "What about you?"

"Don't know, really," replied Tally, looking as evasive as she sounded. And, at that moment, she really didn't know what she would do.

"Suit yourself," Jay told her. "Right, see you, Hugh."

"It's Hugh*ie*," he said, watching her appreciatively as she walked briskly away along the towpath. It was only when she was out of sight that he remembered he'd been going to ask her what her speciality was as a swimmer. He had no doubt at all that she had one.

GOING PLACES

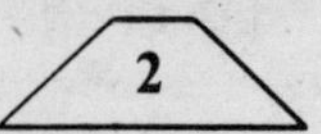

Even Jay was beginning to feel the need for a rest. Kerry had already complained twice that she was tiring and didn't see any point in wearing herself out. So, as they arrived at a relatively level stretch of the steep lane they'd been climbing for some time, Jay signalled her decision by stepping off her cycle, propping it against the hedge and then collapsing full length on the grass verge.

Kerry instantly followed her example. "Don't think I could climb another metre, the way I feel. Honestly, Jay, you'll kill me off one of these days. I'm warning you, so be ready to call 999 for the ambulance."

"If you're dead, you'll need a hearse, not an ambulance," Jay retorted without sympathy. "They don't let corpses travel in ambulances."

Kerry, raising her head a centimetre or two above the grass, asked, "Is that really true or are you just making it up?"

"It's true."

"But how do you know? I mean, do you — did you — know somebody who died and they wouldn't take them in an ambulance?"

"Yes, my grandad — Mum's Dad. I wasn't old enough to know much about it at the time, but it caused a bit of a fuss and my mum still talks about it sometimes if there's been an accident. Anyway, I don't want to talk about it now." She raised one bare leg high in the air and contemplated it from ankle to thigh. "I really think my muscles are getting stronger all the time, you know."

Kerry wrinkled her nose with disapproval. "If I had legs like yours I wouldn't want to risk making

them all knobbly and bunchy with thick muscles. Some models don't have legs as good as yours. You shouldn't spoil them, Jay. You could be a model, you know. You could be famous; have your picture in all the glossy mags and parade for Princess Di at fashion shows!"

"I haven't got the face for a model," Jay pointed out, without any trace of self pity. "Anyway, that's not how I want to be famous. My fame's going to come through swimming, nothing else. That's why it's important to have good leg muscles — your legs have to be as strong as your arms. You should know that, Kerry."

Her friend was sitting up, patting into position the pyramid of blonde hair that was piled on top of her head. "You mean because darling Janet criticizes my — my style? But I don't care as much about winning as you do. Just wish our darling coach would understand that. Who wants piles of medals and dinkie little silver cups and stuff like that? Well, I know *you* do, Jay, but—"

"Only because they'll mean I'm the best at something — my speciality — that's all. I mean, that's all they do, prove your skills. I don't want them for themselves, if you see what I mean. Mum'd only complain about dusting them, anyway. You know what she's like about dust! Look, you've got lots of talent, Kerry. Janet tells everybody you have — well, she tells me, anyway. She only gets mad with you because she thinks you're wasting it by not swimming to the best of your ability, that you don't care."

"That's right, that's what I've just told you: I don't care about swimming, not for medals," said

Kerry, as satisfied as she could be without the aid of a mirror that her hair was now in its rightful position. "I've always liked being in the water and I like being with you. You're my best friend. But my life's never going to be all about swimming is it? I want to go places, see things, do *exciting* things, meet famous people. You don't do all that in a swimming pool, you know."

Jay sat up sharply. "You do if you're world class — well, international class. You might even do it if you're swimming for the county. Top swimmers get invited all over the place, and the best get to the Olympics don't they? Think of all the fanstastic places you'd get to then and—"

"Oh, come on, Jay! You know I'll never be that good and I don't think you will, however much you train and improve. You must know that. O.K. you're the best girl butterflyer in The Club, but if you'd been the best around it would've shown by now. You'd've been picked for the county team at least — *and* the South Region or whatever it's called."

Jay hugged her knees into her chest and scowled. "I could be a late developer. Lots of girls my age — our age — are, you know. Look at Lucie Fortunoff, how she's shot up lately, and *filled out* as my dear mother puts it. Just because I haven't filled out in the same way. Anyway a big bust is a handicap when you're swimming, I reckon."

"But that's all physical development, Jay. And I meant—"

"That's what I'm taking about, physical late development, as well as extra strength and coordination and timing and, oh, I don't know, instinct, like Janet says. All the things she says." She paused, believing she'd convinced herself, whatever effect her words had on Kerry. Then she remembered something. "Listen, remember the last Olympics? Well there was a woman swimmer — woman, mind, not girl — who went back to international swimming after having a baby. And she was really getting on, in her thirties, at least; and she was supposed to be better than ever. So that just shows, Kerry, doesn't it?."

Kerry nodded. "I suppose so. But — well, don't get too carried away Jay. I think you should have something else to, well, look forward to just in case swimming goes wrong on you. You never know, darling Janet might even go off you or decide to go and coach somewhere else. Anything could happen."

The scowl was still there. "I do wish you'd stop calling her 'darling' Janet all the time. You've got into a rut about that. And it's stupid because you don't even like her — and you think she doesn't like you. I know."

"Sorry, but it's only a sort of joke, you know. Honestly, Jay, your sense of humour seems to have gone down the plughole with the bath water — sorry, pool water! Oh come on, Jay, you could try to laugh a bit. It wasn't the world's worst joke."

"I just don't think swimming is a joke at any time. And you won't get coaches more dedicated than Janet, anywhere. You ought to be grateful that she takes such an interest in you. If you were useless she'd have you out of that pool in a hundredth of a second."

Kerry sighed and got to her feet. There were times, she decided, when she preferred to be out on her own and this was quickly becoming one of them. Jay seemed to be obsessed with swimming just now, even more than usual. Kerry wished that something good could happen to her friend, something that would give her a boost as a swimmer. It also occurred to her that if Jay did achieve swimming success then Janet might concentrate all her attention on Jay — which would make life at the pool more enjoyable for Kerry herself.

"Look, I've got to get home — must do some work for that French oral test. I'm not letting Madam-mwe-selle Reynolds bawl me out again for — what did she call it? Oh yeah — *diabolical* pronunciation. Anyway, I'll need good French when I go off and work in Paris at the Salon Sophisticate, *ah oui, ma petite.*"

"Eh?" Jay, still concentrating on her physical improvements, hadn't really been listening. "What are you on about?"

This time Kerry let her laughter roll out. "Honestly, I reckon you're in a terrible state, Jay! A couple of weeks ago you'd have picked up every joke I tried. Now — well, words fail me!"

"Look, are you coming tonight?" Jay wanted to know, having decided that Kerry's present mood was too silly to bother about. "You're not thinking of packing in your swimming, are you? It just wouldn't be the same at The Club without you there."

Her friend looked away, biting at one corner of

her generous mouth, staring down into the valley where they both lived and which was the centre of her life for the moment; but not, she vowed, for ever. She was going to get away from Pennyburn just as soon as it could be managed. She would experience real excitement, meet real people, people who had the same ambitions as herself. She felt she should start preparing for her new life now: preparing by giving up such fruitless pastimes as swimming up and down this lane, up and down that lane, then round and round in circles, supposedly to improve her abilities and thus her value to The Club as a competitor. Yet she didn't want to lose Jay's friendship.

"You *are* packing it in, aren't you?" Jay demanded, real bitterness in her voice. "You've got something else you want to do, haven't you?"

Kerry shook her head, grinning a little lopsidedly at Jay's anguish. "No, I'll give it a go for a bit longer, I suppose. Maybe dear Ja — oh, sorry — maybe our coach will give me a break and actually encourage me instead of finding every fault under the sun with me. Or maybe — hey, how about this — maybe she'll find another victim!"

"Great!" exclaimed Jay, jumping to her feet. Now that she'd won her argument, as she saw it, she was content to follow Kerry's lead and head for home. With a bit of luck she might avoid the mass of jobs that her mother would have piled up for her, though she doubted it. The trouble with living in a boarding house (or a "family hotel" as her mother insisted on on describing it) was that there was always something waiting to be done and somebody waiting for it to be finished.

"See you then, Kerry," she said cheerfully, as they parted by the Post Office. Then she remembered something. "Oh, yeah — might be some new members there tonight. If the ones I've invited turn up."

Kerry braked hard and skidded recklessly. She turned back, her interest unmistakeable. "Oh, who's this then? Are they — fascinating?"

With a wide sweep Jay turned her bike in the direction of home again. "You'll have to come and find out for yourself," she yelled back. "I don't know who *you* would find fascinating, but I think *he* is!"

As soon as she parked her cycle in the shed behind the large Edwardian house where they lived, Jay spotted her mother signalling frantically from the dining-room window. Another urgent job to be done, doubtless. Jay groaned and wished, for the millionth time, that she lived in an ordinary house as a member of an ordinary family that never had a single stranger to stay with them from one year's end to the next. There were times when she wished that she didn't live in Britain at all: that she could emigrate to a hot country where you could swim in the sea all the year round and be happy. There were times, too, when she wanted to surprise Kerry by declaring, "O.K. let's go abroad together, now. Let's just abandon everybody."

"Where *have* you been, Jane?" her mother demanded the moment Jay stepped into the kitchen. "I warned you I might need you this afternoon. You'd no right to go swanning off on your bike, no right at all. Look, Mrs Mercer hasn't come in today. One of her daughters has been rushed in for an emergency op and Mrs Mercer's got to see to her grandchildren. So the beds are still to be made in One, Two and Three — and there's the dusting and Hoovering. Oh, and there's tables to be set and place mats need sponging down and — well, you just get on with that for the moment . . . "

Jay didn't try to argue; there was nothing to be gained from that. If her mother addressed her by her real name then she knew she was out of favour and wouldn't get back into it until she did as she was told. It was a rotten way of treating somebody, Jay believed, but that's the way it was. One day she'd be free and then she could please herself what she did. Usually Mrs Vigar didn't use any name at all in deference to her daughter's wish to be known as Jay, something she couldn't bring herself to say. But anything was better than Jane; Plain Jane as she'd been taunted with at her first school.

Collecting cleaning materials from the tall cupboard on the landing, she set off to tackle Guest Rooms One to Three, thankful that more people hadn't been staying overnight at Homeleigh Hotel ("I know, it's a dreadful pun, *dreadful*," Jay would apologize to whoever commented on the name). It was something she was quite used to because old Mrs Mercer made a habit of responding to crises in her own multi-layered family and leaving her employer, Mrs Vigar, to cope with the hotel business as best as she could. Because Jay's mother insisted on doing all the cooking herself and wouldn't serve convenience foods ("Our guests expect proper home-cooked food here and that's just what they'll get") she was always short of time to do other essential daily jobs when Mrs Mercer wasn't around, for she resolutely refused to employ part-time staff except in the direst emergency.

Making beds was always the worst job of all, which was why Jay neglected making her own unless her mother discovered what she was up to (fortunately Mrs Mercer usually did it for her, thus securing Jay's support when she needed it in most domestic disagreements). Luckily, on this occasion, last night's visitors had been a tidy lot and so the rooms didn't need much sorting out.

As she manipulated the hated Hoover round Number Three she concentrated her thoughts on her swimming and, particularly, her turns: her weakness, as Janet was inclined to say. "You've just got to turn faster — if you don't you're wasting all the advantages you've built up in getting to the wall." Jay recognized the truth of that. She'd thought of a slicker routine and now she was keen to test it out.

"And don't forget to give the cutlery a polish when you come down," her mother yelled from the foot of the stairs. "It's no good having the tables gleaming if the cutlery looks jaded."

Jaded: that was one of her mother's favourite words. Jay couldn't imagine how cutlery could look jaded but plainly her mother could. All that could go wrong now was that she'd have to act as waitress as well as bed maker and cleaner and dust remover and kitchen maid. Waiting was the most familiar role of all and she hated that almost as much as bed making. One day, though, one day she'd be free of all this and famous and she'd stay in top hotels and be kindness itself to the over-worked staff. After all, she would know what they'd had to suffer.

"Look," she said as fiercely as she dared when all the jobs at last were finished, "I've got to be at The Club tonight on time, *got* to be. New members are coming for the first time and, well, Janet wants me to see — see to things . . . "

Amazingly, her mother was smiling. "Well, if Janet wants, Janet must have, mustn't she?" she responded silkily. "Oh, it's all right, love, you don't have to act as waitress tonight. Mrs Mercer's arranged for one of her granddaughters to come over for a couple of hours — sounds a competent sort from what I'm told. So you can have your supper now and get off when you're ready. I'm grateful for what you've done."

Jay blinked. Sometimes, just sometimes, her mother really seemed to consider her feelings and get things just right. The one thing she got right all the time was the meals she cooked. "The food at your place is *divine*," Kerry would say. "Honestly, the French hotels would give millions and millions of francs to have someone like your mother in their kitchens."

Jay, who'd been made aware by Janet how very important diet was to a swimmer's progress, couldn't disagree with that view. But now, before she set off for a vital training session, all she wanted was a glass of milk and a Mars bar.

There'd always be something good in the pantry when she got home again.

"So what's on tonight then?" Hughie's father asked him, as he headed purposefully for the garage where he kept his racing bike with its special tyres and assortment of gears.

"Going to show 'em I'm the champion," replied Hughie, not even breaking his stride as he passed his father who was efficiently cleaning every part of his precious lawnmower in readiness for its winter hibernation.

"Oh, I realize that," said Mr McGavin with mock resignation. "I just wondered which lot were going to have the benefit of seeing what a fantastic performer you are. The basketball boys...the tennis set...the marathon men...the—"

"Nah, none of that lot," was the dismissive answer. "Going swimming tonight — showing these girls I met that I can stay underwater longer than a submarine. Oh yeah, and move faster than a torpedo."

"That's different." Mr McGavin's surprise was genuine, although he had long ago come to terms with his only son's glowing self image. "Look, you're not going in the river, are you? I've told you before how dangerous—"

"Nah, it's a proper swimming pool — proper club, too. Called The Swimming Club this girl Jay says. She's sort of one of the organizers, I think." Hughie, having paused for several seconds, now launched himself into a sprint. "Must dash. Don't want 'em to think I'm not turning up; that I'm chicken."

Mr McGavin managed a laugh. "Hughie, nobody who's ever met you would ever think that for a second!"

But Hughie, of course, was no longer listening.

Tally had been uncertain all day about whether she would go to The Swimming Club. She sensed that Jay didn't even want her there: that the invitation she'd thrown out was really aimed just at Hughie. Or perhaps Jay was such a great swimmer that she would beat any other girl out of sight. Certainly she'd looked pretty good in the water when she thought she might have to rescue Hughie.

Yet Tally herself was a more than capable swimmer. At school there wasn't anyone who could compete with her; but then, she didn't know what her own standard really was. As she'd told Jay, no one at her school was very interested in swimming, let alone in competitions. Jay had admitted that she'd won prizes and so perhaps she was really brilliant at everything: butterfly, breaststroke, backstroke, crawl.

The only way Tally could really find out was by competing against her. But what if Jay absolutely murdered her at everything, left her for dead? She didn't feel she could face that kind of humiliation. So why risk it? Jay had struck her as being smug enough already. An easy triumph over a new girl would simply allow her to add to her high opinion of herself. She and the insufferable Hughie would make a pretty good pair, Tally told herself.

And yet — if she didn't give herself a chance of swimming in competition she never would discover whether she had real talent. The coach might spot her potential and want to train her for top class competition. She might get to the area finals and then be chosen for the county and . . . Well, all sorts of wonderful things could happen to her. She would be on the road to fame.

Tally had ambitions she would never disclose to anyone; well, not to anyone she hadn't known for a long time and could trust completely. At present, there was no one in her life in that category. She had a sister but they didn't have anything in common at all apart from family ties. Their interests were, as their mother acknowledged when talking about them to acquaintances, poles apart. Although their appearances were similar they didn't think alike or share any friends. Corinne was a couple of years younger than Tally but she was the one with a circle of admirers, a gang of mates that she spent every spare minute with outside their home. Tally hated to admit it, even to herself, but there wasn't any one at all she could describe as a true friend. And that was something she missed enormously. Perhaps, though, at The Swimming Club she would meet the person she needed in her life.

Just before she knew she'd be called down for tea Tally sat in her bedroom, reading a novel, still undecided about what she would do that evening. She wished she had a family as interesting as the one she was reading about: this girl in New York had a great sense of humour and a cute little brother and, it seemed likely, her first boyfriend who obviously thought she was terrific — and parents who really cared about their children and didn't just think about themselves. Tally sighed. But before she could start on the next chapter her mother yelled up the stairs.

"Your tea'll be on the table in less than thirty seconds, so I want you down here *immediately*. Oh, and your Aunt Liz has arrived and she wants a word with you, Tally. So, come on."

That was the moment Tally decided where she was going to spend her evening: at The Swimming Club. If there was one person in the world she couldn't stand, it was her mother's sister. Aunt Liz not only treated her like an infant but like an infant who was also an idiot, someone who had to be coo-ed over and petted and, of course, not listened to for a moment. Always she managed to arrive at their house just as a meal was being served. Never did she wait for an invitation to join them; she simply sat down at the table as if she lived there and was entitled to share in everything. From that point onwards the conversation was what she wanted it to be.

"I won't be eating much; hardly anything, really," announced Tally as she sat down. "I've got to go out soon — swimming. At The Club."

"Oh," said Aunt Liz, eyes widening, "that's different, lovey. Now when I was your age and started swimming . . .."

SOLO SWIM

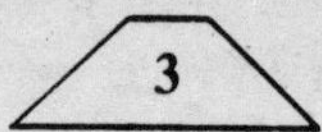

Hughie liked the look of the red door in Rule Street. For one thing, red was his favourite colour and the glossiness of the paint suggested that everything behind it was new and smart and exciting. He knew The Swimming Club would be delighted to welcome him as a member: they'd be thrilled to have someone with his outstanding ability in their ranks. Probably they'd been searching for a star performer. Well, that star was now about to walk through the entrance. The crimsom-coloured door opened to his touch.

The knife-sharp, antiseptic smell of chlorine reached him immediately even though there was no sight yet of the pool; that was along a corridor and down a shallow flight of stone steps. It was bigger than he'd expected with several rows of tiered seats on either of the long sides and, above them, plate-glass windows of viewing areas. Showers and changing rooms were located at the far end of the pool from where he stood, taking in the impressive scale of The Swimming Club. But what surprised him more than anything was that there wasn't another person to be seen anywhere. Even the water looked as if it had never been disturbed by so much as a single human toe.

Although a trifle disappointed by the absence of an official welcoming committee, Hughie wasn't going to let that spoil things; now he was here he might as well make the most of it and enjoy the freedom of the pool before everyone else jumped in. After checking out a few of the changing rooms he went back to the first one he'd looked at for it was impressively bigger than the rest and even contained its own washbasin and shower unit. He ignored the fact that it said "Private" on the door.

He hung his clothes very neatly on hangers and pegs. Although he'd been accused of having many faults untidiness wasn't one of them. Hughie liked to know where things were when he wanted them: time spent searching for missing articles was time wasted, in his view. A cupboard above the washbasin contained some interesting pots and bottles and he had a sniff at several: one in particular provided an intoxicating smell and he decided he'd splash some of that stuff on after his swim. But no! Why wait until then? He might as well try it now and improve the smell of the pool.

Jauntily, he left the changing room, its door key now secreted in the inner pocket of his red-and-blue trunks, and returned to the pool, which was still completely deserted. But that didn't trouble Hughie. It was, he felt, a pity that there

was no one to see his spectacular entry into the water, a curious, spiralling, sideways movement from a standing position on the side of the bath. It was something he'd once tried out on the river bank when demonstrating to a bunch of scoffers from a rival school just how a guy would "hit the deck — well, water then" after being struck by a hail of bullets. They had, indeed, been impressed because, naturally, it took him quite a while to resurface and half of them were convinced that he'd committed suicide. Now he was trying to improve on his technique by spinning round 360 degrees before actually touching the water.

The temperature was perfect and Hughie revelled in the opportunity to swim wherever he wanted without being impeded by anyone. He could really get up a cracking speed; but it was the submerged surges that he enjoyed the most. Soon, though, he would get bored: he needed either an audience or competition or someone to annoy.

After executing a couple of dolphin-like U-turns Hughie decided it was time to go in for a bit of springboard diving. He might come up (or rather go down, he grinned to himself) with some more novelty twists. Hughie broke the surface — and discovered that someone was waiting for him with a fierce glare.

"What on earth do you think you're doing?" demanded the tall, youngish woman in a pale blue tracksuit. Her tone would have chilled most people of Hughie's age. He just grinned as if he knew her well and had been expecting her arrival.

"Just having a bit of a swim — and so I'm not

on earth, am I? But it's a bit boring on your own. When're the rest coming?"

Janet Gainfield wasn't used to receiving flippant answers to her questions, or to having her authoritative attitude ignored when she was plainly displeased by that person's conduct.

"Who are you and who let you in here?" were the next two questions which were asked, if possible, in an even harsher tone.

Hughie couldn't understand what she was on about; he guessed who she was and so she should know that Jay had invited him to The Club. It wasn't his fault if everybody else turned up late. Was he supposed just to hang around and ignore all that tempting water until he was told he could jump in? All that was going through his mind but, for once, he had the sense not to put his thoughts into unwelcome words. He had an idea that this young woman could get very tough with anyone who really opposed her.

"I'm Hughie McGavin and it was a girl called Jay that invited me here and nobody let me in because there was nobody around when I arrived. The door was open so I thought it was O.K. to walk in." He kept himself lazily afloat as he told her all that and he tried to look pleasant.

For once, Janet wasn't sure how to react. This boy with the cheeky style sounded as though he might be telling the truth; and he also gave the impression that he might be quite useful in the water. And The Club could do with more boys as members. On the other hand, it was unlike Jim Tordoff, the caretaker, to leave doors open so that anyone could wander in at will from the street and help themselves to a swim. She supposed she ought to see where he was.

"Well next time, if there is a next time, you wait until everyone else is here before going in the water," she said in a fairly conciliatory manner as she fished in her shoulder bag for some keys. "You sure you didn't see the caretaker? Fattish little man with gingery sort of hair and — oh, and really big hands."

"Nope! Told you. I saw nobody. Look, why—"

"Right, well I've got to find him. You'd better get out and have a rub down. We don't normally go in the water as soon as we arrive. There are exercises and discussions first. We have a very professional approach to swimming at this Club, so you'd better learn that if you want to join us."

She moved away, heading towards the changing rooms. Hughie wrinkled his nose at her back, rolled his eyes heavenwards and sank out of sight. He decided he might as well enjoy life while he could: he had an idea he wouldn't be spending much more time in coach Janet's desirable swimming pool.

In only a matter of moments she was back again, arriving at a very fast speed, and trailing her was the fattish little man she'd found having one of his secret smokes by the rear entrance.

"You, there!" she yelled. "Whatever your name is. Come out at once! Of all the infernal cheek . . . "

Hughie, only half suspecting what was bothering her, rose gracefully through the water to emerge in the very centre of the pool. Janet, he saw, was holding aloft a grey-and-blue checked sweater.

"Is this yours?" she yelled.

"I guess so."

"Don't misuse words with me! Is it yours or isn't it? Come on, a straight answer."

"Yeah, but—"

"Then what was it doing in *my* changing room; my personal, private changing room, actually marked 'Private' on the door? How dare you break into my room!"

Hughie grimaced and thought about sinking from sight again, but he realized that wouldn't really help the situation. "Didn't know it was your room, did I? I mean, it didn't say so on the door."

"Just because it didn't have my name on the door doesn't mean you can go barging in wherever you like," Janet went on relentlessly, the caretaker standing stolidly beside her, no expression of any kind on his heavy face. "It says 'Private' and that should be enough for anybody — it would be for anybody but a, a trickster, a delinquent, like you! I've a good mind to chuck all your stuff in the pool and let you fish it out."

There was nothing Hughie felt he could say. It did occur to him it was a good thing he wasn't standing beside her, for then she might have detected the stuff he had sprayed over himself; no doubt it belonged to her and she'd label him a thief as well as a trickster, whatever that was supposed to mean.

"Anyway, you can get out of that pool this instant!" she ordered. "If you don't, I'll come in there myself and throw you out. So—"

At that moment Jay and Kerry came through the door and stopped dead as they heard Janet Gainfield's furious comments and saw Hughie reclining on his back in the centre of the pool. But he didn't remain in that position any longer. If he was going to be chucked out of The Club before he was even in it then he might as well make the most of his last soak. So, stone like, he suddenly sank from sight.

Janet was heatedly interrogating Jay, who hadn't said a word so far, when she suddenly realized that the boy hadn't resurfaced. Momentarily, that silenced her as she stared, almost transfixed, at the spot where she'd last seen him.

"Oh, goodness!" she exclaimed. "Something's wrong. He's—"

"No, he's O.K. Janet, I know he is," interrupted Jay, as the coach hastily started to strip off her tracksuit. "Hughie's got fantastic lungs. He can stay down for ages. It's a trick of his to make you think he's — well, drowned."

Janet gave her a disbelieving look but she knew Jay well enough not to question that statement. She'd already sensed, from her first sighting of Hughie, that he had something of the natural affinity with water that many top swimmers possessed. But her anger over his insolent conduct had temporarily pushed that out of her mind. Now she experienced a tingle of excitement: could this boy with the spiky hair and bold eyes be the kind of swimmer every coach wanted to find?

"There he is!" yelled Kerry, unable to contain

her own excitement, as Hughie popped up on the far side of the pool. She had already heard a good deal from Jay about this boy with the extraordinary underwater talent but she hadn't expected to see him demonstrate it so soon. "He looks — well, *normal*, really."

Hughie, for the moment unaware of the effect he'd created, decided it was time to go. The coach still looked capable of carrying out her threats. He turned to swim to the side.

"Hang on a minute, Hughie!" Janet called to him. "Stay in the water, please."

Hughie blinked, and not just because he'd got water in his eyes. Moments ago this fierce young woman was trying to tear him to shreds; now she'd even remembered his name and said "please". It was the last word that kept him in the pool: before that he'd been determined to put as much distance as possible between himself and The Swimming Club coach.

"Is backstroke what you usually swim?" she was asking from just above him.

"Well, yeah. I mean, I can stay under longest doing that." He paused, but couldn't resist a typical boast. "But I'm a great crawler and my breaststroke's not bad!"

"Right, let's see you in real action, then," said Janet, pulling a stopwatch from her pocket. "I want you to do a couple of lengths of the pool, starting from that end. Start properly with your hands on the rail and go when I blow my whistle. Just go as fast as you can and make a good turn. Just imagine you're out to beat the world champion, O.K.?"

By now, several other girls, and a few boys, had arrived and were standing beside Jay and Kerry, waiting to see what would happen. Tally came in on her own and was going to speak to Jay when she saw that it was Hughie who was the centre of attention. So she, too, joined the rest of the spectators, having a better idea than most of them what might happen. There was already a buzz of excitement among those who'd been members for some time. It was unheard of for the coach to put someone through his paces before the start of a normal evening training session.

Hughie, thrilled by the idea of racing against a world champion, took up the position Janet had indicated, gave everybody the benefit of his biggest grin and waited impatiently for the signal.

Janet deliberately stretched the waiting period just to see how this confident newcomer would react to a first touch of discipline. But, to both their surprise, he made no attempt to jump the gun. The coach nodded approvingly to herself. She was praying that everything else about his swim would turn out to be as good: but it was potential that she was looking for at this stage.

His eagerness to display instant brilliance caught him out almost as soon as the whistle shrilled. His push off wasn't firm enough and he failed to take in enough air for the initial submerged stretch. Having to come up sooner than intended, he lost the rhythm he normally achieved and rolled awkwardly. But the second intake was right and his progress under the surface drew gasps from those who'd never seen him in action before. Now he was swimming with rare concentration, determined to show Janet he was the best backstroker she'd ever seen.

Janet Gainfield's computer of a mind was registering all the technical errors the boy was committing but none of them mattered for the moment; she would deal with those at the right time. She had never yet met a young swimmer whose technique couldn't be improved by her methods of teaching. But she winced as he attempted one of the most cumbersome turns she'd ever seen. Plainly, Hughie hadn't had a lesson in his life. Yet his time was still astonishingly good.

He bounced into the wall at the point where he'd set off from and, shaking the water from his face, grinned triumphantly across at Janet. In his own mind he was a hero: a true world champion might have beaten him but surely no else in his own age group.

"What did you think of that, then?" he yelled.

Janet smiled. None of her pupils would have dared ask a question like that. They'd have waited, probably with some anxiety, for her to speak first, to deliver her verdict in her own way. Hughie, it was clear, was from a different mould. But he was just what she wanted. In her experience, no one reached the top without confidence, drive and personality — and dedication. Hughie, she suspected, possessed the first three attributes. Only time would tell whether he was able to develop genuine determination to go as far as his talent would take him.

"Not bad, but you could do better — a lot

better," she told him. "I take it you've never swum in a competition?"

He shook his head, emphatically. "Never thought about it. D'you think I could win, then?"

Kerry giggled, and waited for the sort of scorching comment the coach usually delivered when someone was a bit cocky. But Kerry had never worked out that Janet was inclined to be easier on boys.

"I wouldn't be surprised," was the reply that surprised not only Kerry Paynter, "*provided* you put in lots of hard work and you're willing to learn; to listen to good advice. And you really do have plenty to learn, Hughie. That said, then I believe you've got the ability to do well."

Hughie was delighted. He'd never doubted that ability but it was always good to hear someone else's view; and he was shrewd enough to know that people like Janet — teachers, for example — nearly always understated things in order to make you work harder. They didn't like to ladle out too much praise in case you got the idea you could get what you wanted without effort. In spite of all his talents at different sports, Hughie McGavin hadn't yet won anything at any of them. Now, it seemed, he was on the way . . .

"What've I got to do, then?" he wanted to know, eager as always to get into action again.

"I'll tell you all about that later on. Now's not the time. I do have a responsibility to the other Club members, you know," she said, smiling brightly. "By the way, now that you've heard you could be good enough to win competitions, I take it you *do* want to join The Swimming Club."

"Oh sure, *definitely*." Already he was beginning to imagine what it would be like to have, in his bedroom, a shelf full of swimming trophies and medals and huge photos on the walls of his triumphs. "Does it, er, cost anything?"

"Well, nothing I'm sure you can't afford for what you're going to get out of it. But we'll deal with that later, too. First, though, you've got to do something else, something rather important." She was still smiling as she said it.

"Oh sure" — eagerly.

"You get out of the pool and you go to that changing room you hijacked and you get your things out of there! And, in future, remember that it's my room, not yours." She'd stopped smiling, but even Hughie could tell she wasn't as angry as she sounded. "Martin, here, will show you which changing room you can have. You'd better have a rub down, too. You won't be going back into the pool just yet. I believe I have another possible new member to talk to. So—"

"But—"

"No buts, Hughie. At this Swimming Club the coach always has the last word. That's something you'd better remember. Now, girls, I think it's time you got changed — and then . . .."

URGE TO COMPETE

Jay, adjusting her rainbow costume for maximum comfort, strolled towards the pool with Kerry, who was thinking that if Janet got mad at her again tonight she'd pack up swimming completely and this time Jay wouldn't be able to persuade her to change her mind.

"So what do you think of my new recruit, then?" Jay inquired, tilting her head towards Tally who was sporting a black-and-gold outfit. Jay had greeted Tally when she arrived but they hadn't had much to say to each other, mostly because they'd all been magnetized by Hughie's performance.

"Well, she's thinner than I thought she was when she had her clothes on. But maybe those vertical stripes help. They're supposed to, aren't they, if you want to look sort of sleek." She turned her face away so that Tally wouldn't see her laughter. "But anyone'd look thin standing beside Lucie Fortunoff!"

"And Tally'll be bored to death already because Lucie'll be filling her in on the details of what her latest diet consists of," Jay said, sharing a laugh. "No, but I mean, what do you think she'll be like as a swimmer? Any good?"

Kerry considered this after a covert glance at the pair now dipping ankles into the water to test the temperature. "Dunno, really. Could be anything, couldn't she? Probably she goes in for a very elegant, ladylike breastroke. But if she does dear Jan — oh, sorry, Jay — just plain Janet, well, Janet will get after her to swim harder, swim *harder*, that's it!"

She tried to keep her voice down during that fierce imitation but one or two of the other girls looked across at them and giggled. They guessed that one day Kerry would want to get her own back on their coach.

Having allocated various kicking and swim-with-one-arm exercises to the boys, Janet now turned her attention to the girls, most of whom believed they knew exactly what their programme would be. They were wrong.

"You lot keep complaining that you never get enough competition swimming, that you don't meet other swimmers," the coach declared. As usual, she had changed into white shorts and white T-shirt bearing the words "The Swimming Club" in red across the chest; an outfit that always seemed to emphasise her height. "Well, you should be pleased to hear that I've fixed up a challenge match with the Outlane Swimming Club for a week next Thursday. Could be that we'll get some sort of sponsorship for it so that we can provide a few medals and trophies — and, of course, a challenge cup for the winners to hold for a year. Because we want it to be an annual event. Don't quite know yet whether that'll be possible but Miss Sanders — she's their coach — and I are working on it. So, any comments?"

"Oh, great!" and, "Hey, that's terrific!" were the exclamations that greeted the news; but nobody actually thought to praise their coach for having the initiative to arrange the event, which was the sort of disappointment Janet was used to at The Club. Jay was the one who asked the important question.

"Will everybody be competing — or just some of us?"

"Probably just some of you," replied Janet, approving of Jay's tactful phrasing. "But that isn't decided yet. Anyway, we want to field our strongest team in every event. Outlane are a pretty good club. But there's also another reason for putting on a good display."

She paused for a moment but no one put the question into words. "All being well," she continued, "some good judges will be present; county selectors very likely. So I don't have to spell it out that if anyone catches their eye . . .."

It was exactly what Jay had been hoping for and her eyes widened in delight. She knew that if it came down to choosing the strongest swimmer in the various events she would be first in the butterfly and a certainty for the medley relay. Probably she would get the vote in the breastroke, too.

"Great, isn't it?" she said, turning keenly to Kerry. "You'll be in the first pick and then — hey, what is it?"

"Won't be able to make it," explained Kerry, who had been shaking her head as Jay's enthusiasm grew. "There's a very special hairdressing demonstration at the Cavendish that night. Must be there. Never know who I might meet. All sorts of possibilities. Might even offer myself as a model. I mean—"

"Kerry, you can go to see that sort of thing any old time. A challenge match like this, well . . .."

Even as she talked, though, Jay was viewing Kerry's likely absence with mixed feelings. Her best friend was quite capable of beating her in any swimming event, apart from butterfly, if she put her mind to it; so without her there she would have one fewer rival to worry about. On the other hand, Kerry's companionship was important to her. Jay didn't have a close relationship with any of the other Club members — or anyone else at school, come to that.

By now Janet had turned her attention to the newcomer, asking about her swimming experience and her stroke preferences. Tally gave the impression of being withdrawn, even sullen, but Janet put that down to shyness. The girl had a good build and the height that could be a great advantage if she possessed any real talent. Once she'd allocated tasks to the rest of the girls she instructed Tally to move over to the clear lane.

"You did say you'd had a go at butterfly?" she checked.

Tally nodded. "Sort of, but it was harder than I

thought so I didn't bother too much. And nobody else was doing it."

"Well, it doesn't suit everybody, I know," Janet agreed. "Like everything else, you've got to have the timing and coordination and, well push. Tally, you've got good shoulders so I'd like you to see what you can do now. Just a couple of lengths. Don't worry about the turn. If it's for you, the fly, we'll soon smooth that off."

It wasn't at all what Tally wanted to do. She'd come to The Club to improve her skills, not experiment with something she'd hardly ever tried. So far she wasn't enjoying herself at all. Jay, who'd invited her in the first place, had scarcely even spoken to her. All she seemed to do was whisper to her blonde friend, Kerry, and the two of them, Tally suspected, were just waiting to have a good laugh at her. Tally was also conscious of her slimness: was she *too* thin? Well, she certainly was compared to Lucie Fortunoff, but then Lucie was obviously obsessed by food. She was thinner than Jay, too, but not by much.

She didn't know what to think of Janet, except that she was a bit bossy — but that was to be expected. She was also very attractive and it occurred to Tally that she and the coach were really quite similar in appearance if you made allowances for the big difference in ages. But that wouldn't guarantee that they'd get on well together. Tally and her sister Corinne had the same features and they couldn't stand each other.

As she climbed out of the pool and made her way to her starting point she saw that the coach was already setting her stopwatch. It made Tally

think that even though she knew she wouldn't be any good at real butterfly swimming she ought to try her best. After all, she didn't want them to think she was so hopeless there was no point in her joining The Swimming Club.

She was moving even as the whistle sounded and entered the water like an arrow. It was a start of which any swimmer would have been proud and Tally's glide carried her down the lane and into the first thrust of her shoulders in the butterfly movement. The kick down was strong and regular and it was all being achieved by instinct. But she knew she was doing well.

As Janet feared, the turn was clumsy and she touched with only one hand with one shoulder somehow twisted below the other; but after that the momentum was regained and Tally completed her second length with rising confidence. She hadn't known she could swim like that using the butterfly. Shaking the water from her face, she sought the coach's opinion.

"That was good," Janet told her, deliberately not giving rein to her true feelings. This was astonishing: two new members in one evening and two swimmers with real prospects of success. Well, at the very least, high potential. And this girl didn't even believe she could do the butterfly! "Look, how do you feel about it, about trying it out again?"

For the moment, Tally didn't know how to respond, and that was why she looked away and caught the expression on Jay's face. She thought it showed annoyance, but it could have been envy or worry. One way or another, Tally's performance had affected the other girl, and Tally suddenly felt pleased with herself. She remembered, too, that Janet had said something nice about her shoulders, and Tally had long thought that her shoulders were a bit slopey and knobbly.

"Well, it was O.K. I mean, I enjoyed it," she said, cautiously, trying to avoid looking at Jay again but wondering what was going on behind those dark brown brooding eyes.

"Fine," said the coach, "fine. So do you think you could manage that again?"

"What, now do you mean?"

Janet nodded encouragingly. "Yes, if you really feel up to it. We'll give you a moment's rest and then perhaps you and Jay could swim together. Jay is our butterfly expert."

Tally didn't know what was meant by this idea. "What, race each other, do you mean?"

The coach hesitated. This new girl undeniably had a sharp brain. A race wasn't at all what she had in mind for them at the moment because Jay would win that easily and Janet didn't want Tally to suffer any discouragement at this stage. But a test might reveal something interesting. She had also seen that Jay was aware of what was going on. Jay hadn't mentioned anything at all to her about Tally's prowess as a swimmer so, presumably, this performance in the butterfly was a surprise to her, too. A surprise that she might not welcome.

By now Tally had climbed out of the pool and Janet moved round to put her arm loosely round her shoulders, a gesture that didn't escape Jay.

"Not a race, no, we won't gain anything from that, not tonight. Your technique needs plenty of refinements before you can think of racing."

She paused and signalled to Jay to come over and join them. But all her attention was still on Tally. "Look, I don't want to give you too much to remember to start with but if you could try to keep flatter in the water that would be good, try to keep your body tilted really well forward. It would help, too, if you pushed your chin forward, really thrust it forward as if you were trying to plough a furrow through the surface of the pool. Got the idea?"

"Oh yes, sure, I'll try to remember all that," Tally replied, glad to be getting all this personal attention. Suddenly, things had started to go well for her.

Janet was now talking to Jay, telling her what she had in mind: it wasn't intended to be a race but she did want her and Tally to swim a couple of lengths together using the butterfly. "It'll give me a chance to see whether we've got another candidate for this event when we meet Outlane. And we want to give the best account of ourselves that we can."

Jay, with a sideways glance at Tally, nodded that she understood. But if this wasn't a race what was it? If the coach wanted to find out how good Tally was then the only way she could do it was to test her against The Club's best butterflyer: herself. So she would have to swim at her best to prove that Tally simply wasn't in her league. Then she thought of something else. If she made Tally look absolutely useless then the other girl probably wouldn't join their Club and Jay wouldn't qualify for a bonus payment. Perhaps the best thing to do, therefore, would be to win, but not too easily.

In her eagerness to make a good start Jay, beginning to lose balance on her steeply-curved launching position, was moving before the whistle sounded; and Tally, who hadn't been told anything about the position she should take up, was slow into the water. But Janet didn't bother to order a re-start. She would be able to judge Tally's talent even with a late start.

Jay's powered glide carried her into a good lead from the moment she broke the surface. Her rhythm was quickly established and she had the adrenalin of competition flowing through her body.

It took Tally half the length of the pool to develop any sort of fluency in her arm and leg movements. There was a lot to remember. Jay's flying start had unnerved rather than irritated her. It made her think that she herself was slow and disorganized and she didn't like that. It felt good to compete, and she suddenly knew she had the will to win. She was determined to impress Janet Gainfield. Gradually she developed a correct breathing pattern as shoulders and head went down, up, down, up.

"Come on, Tally, come on!" she urged herself fiercely. "You can do it, you can do it, you can do it."

It was scarcely possible for her to switch any of her attention to the swimmer ahead of her. She knew it was what she herself did that mattered,

not anything else. But by getting closer and closer she would cause her opponent (as she now thought of Jay) to worry about her.

Tally was still well behind at the turn and that, she knew, would give extra heart to Jay. But Tally had an instinctive tactical awareness that Janet Gainfield would soon consider another prime asset in the make up of the tall, sleek newcomer.

Her turn was a little better than her first effort when she was swimming solo and, naturally, Jay gained a further advantage with her slick, well-practised double-handed routine. It allowed her to see that she was well ahead of her opponent and she smiled her satisfaction even as her head went into the water again.

But that was the last moment in which she could rejoice. For, metre by metre, Tally began to catch up. She had already decided that it was on the second length that she'd have to attack if, as she expected, Jay was well ahead of her by then. Jay would be concentrating on her own stroke and, having noted that Tally was trailing her, perhaps just thinking about how much she'd win by. And Tally was right in all that. Without realizing it, Jay did ease off a little — just as Tally was increasing her own efforts.

If she'd been able to show her true feelings about the scene she was witnessing, Janet would have rubbed her hands with glee. It was all turning out very much as she'd hoped. Tally could, one day, be very good indeed. True, she had lots of rough edges but that was to be expected; as an experienced coach she knew how to smooth them off. Then she would discover just how good this girl was. The prospect was exciting.

Kerry was watching almost as keenly. She could see that Tally was reducing Jay's lead quite rapidly and she wanted to yell encouragement to her best friend. But she'd heard Janet tell Tally that it wasn't a race and so she kept silent. She just hoped that Jay had something in reserve because she would absolutely hate it if she were beaten, especially by an unknown, someone she was introducing to The Club. It could all turn out to be rather embarrassing.

Kerry's belief, though, that Jay would keep something in reserve was justified. For the leader had now sensed that her opponent was in close pursuit. She risked a glance — and immediately put everything into her swim.

That extra power and experience carried Jay to the winning post in first place. Tally, who'd just begun to believe that she could win after all, was dismayed to see her rival pull away in the closing stages; and she no longer had the energy or the experience to fight back.

"Well done, both of you!" Janet enthused diplomatically. "I told you it wasn't a race but you just about turned it into one. Still, if that shows how keen you both are, then good. How d'you feel Tally?"

"Oh, O.K. thanks," replied the runner up, still out of breath and still uncertain how she should regard her own performance. She knew she couldn't have gone any faster or kept going any longer at that speed; but she had begun to feel quite confident about the butterfly by the end of the race. Most important of all, though, was that she had got so close to winning. For she was aware that Jay was regarded as the best at the butterfly among the girls at The Swimming Club.

"Well, I think you should go and have a shower and a rub down now," Janet told her. "You've done enough for one session. I'm very impressed and I think you could have success at swimming before too long. I take it, by the way, that you do want to join The Club?"

"Oh yes, please!"

"Fine. I'll give you the entry form and all those details before you go. And we'll have a talk about a training programme geared specially to your needs."

As Tally departed for the changing rooms, Janet raised her eyebrows at Jay. "Well, what was going on out there, then? I thought I told you we weren't treating it as a race?"

Jay thought she managed to convey astonishment quite well. "A race? *I* wasn't racing, Janet. Just giving Tally a lead, that's all. I mean, she finished fairly close to me, didn't she?"

"You know she did — because she's going to be a good competitor, that girl. Look, we're not going to discuss it now. Go and get changed and we'll have a word before you go. We need to talk about the Outlane challenge. I can't be too late away myself tonight. Got to go and see Claire Sanders to start fixing details."

Jay was doing rather more thinking than talking as she and Kerry showered together but, as she watched her best friend fashion her blond tresses into a clever waterfall effect, she asked what she thought of Tally's performance. For a few moments Kerry didn't reply. She wondered just how honest she should be on this occasion.

"Pretty good, really, cosidering she's supposed to have no experience of the butterfly," she replied, having decided that no good purpose would be served by saying anything else. "But she'll be good for you, Jay. I mean, if she keeps pushing you then you'll improve, won't you? You've said plenty of times that we could do with more talent in The Club. Well, I suspect Tally is going to provide some."

"I think you could be right," was Jay's sole comment, much to Kerry's surprise. "Look, while you're finishing off your fantastic hairdo I'll see what Janet wants."

The coach had decided she ought to leave straight away after all and was just on the point of locking her door (the spare key having been earlier retrieved from Hughie) when Jay turned up. "Sorry, Jay," she apologized with one of her winning smiles, "but I've got to dash. So we'll have our chat at the weekend, O.K. Oh, and don't worry about your bounty money for getting Hughie and Tally to join. I'll see it's paid next time. And — oh, Tally! Did you want something special?"

Janet had just been turning away, eager to rush down the corridor, when she caught sight of Tally, standing open mouthed, a few metres away. There was no doubt in Janet's mind, or Jay's either, that she'd heard every word that had been said.

Tally blinked and came out of her trance. "I'd

just started off home when I thought of something," she started to explain, looking distinctly uncomfortable. "I mean, I never asked about next week. Is it, will it be, just all right to turn up again at the same time? I know you said to bring my joining money and that form I've to fill in but well . . . "

"Of course, of course," Janet said firmly, hoping to reassure her. "Sorry I didn't make things clear to you. We *always* meet Tuesdays at six thirty whatever else we've arranged for the rest of the week. Yes, see you then, Tally."

Then, after a quick exchange of glances with Jay, the coach departed, swinging her sports bag in a rather exaggerated fashion. Tally, too, set off for the exit, but not before giving Jay a strange look.

Jay, waiting now for Kerry, stared after them. She wondered what was going through Tally's mind at that moment.

CONKERED!

Hughie was feeling pleased with himself, a not unfamiliar emotion for him. He'd been taking part in an after-school basketball training session and Mr Stoker's praise for Hughie's energy and vision, as he expressed it, had been quite lavish. Normally, Firebrand, as most of the squad had taken to calling their PE teacher, didn't hand out compliments to anyone. What Hughie didn't know was that by praising him Firebrand was hoping to galvanize another player, a rival of Hughie's, into putting more effort into his work in future. That was one of the coach's typical ploys.

As he meandered along New Walk, still contemplating future triumphs on the basketball court, a huge stick, falling through the branches of one of the trees that lined the broad pathway, dropped just in front of him, just missing his head. Then he spotted two younger boys standing beside one of the old trees just ahead, plainly up to no good and just as plainly trying to avoid catching his eye.

"Hey, what's going on?" he yelled at them, before picking up the heavy stick. "Did you chuck this? It could've killed me, you crazy idiots!"

Then he recognized them as Dominic and Matthew, boys he had known at their junior school where, even then, they had been in awe of him. His attitude softened and he saw from the scatterings of broken shells and twigs and snapped branches all along the path what they had been trying to do.

"No luck with any conkers, then?" he enquired jovially, remembering his own great successes of a couple of years ago. He glanced towards the higher branches of the nearest horse chestnut but could spot no tempting targets.

Matthew, red haired and chubby and with something of Hughie's own outgoing manner, held out his hand to display a collection of conkers, not one of which was any larger than a blackbird's egg. "Those are all we could find," he said, dolefully. "Other lads have got the best."

"Yeah, you couldn't beat a dandelion with any of them," Hughie confirmed, still eyeing the trees around him. "You'll have to swap something you own for somebody else's champion conker if you want to get into good fights. When I was—"

"There's a good bunch up there, Hughie." Dominic broke in. He was a thin-faced boy with dark, eager eyes and he was pointing to a tangle of branches high up the tree ahead of them. "There'd be some great conkers in that lot. Bound to be.

But — well, you couldn't dislodge them by chucking anything. Too many other branches in the way."

"You'd have to *climb* up there," Matthew pointed out, using exactly the words Dominic wanted to hear. "But I'm not tall enough to try it — and you aren't, either, Nic."

"Height's not that important," Hughie declared immediately. "You've got to be agile, that's what really counts. I could get up there, I reckon. No danger."

"Oh, thanks, Hughie," rejoiced Dominic, his eyes positively gleaming. "D'you want us to give you a hand to start you off? I mean, it's quite a way to the first strong branch, isn't it?"

Hughie's assessment of what was needed didn't take a second. "O.K. If you two link arms and push yourself against the trunk of the tree I'll just nip up using you as a ladder. No problem. Come on, let's go. Can't spend all night here. Got plenty to do at home."

The younger boys exchanged worried looks at the prospect of being used as a climbing frame but Hughie smartly pushed them into the required position for his ascent.

Dominic winced as Hughie's left foot planted itself firmly on to his shoulder but, of course, it didn't remain there. With a confident jump Hughie was able to grasp the lowest branch and haul himself into the heart of the tree. The trickiest part of the operation, however, still lay ahead. For the most desirable grouping of chestnuts was still out of reach, dangling from an upward curving branch well over to his right. To get within arm's length he needed to negotiate an awkwardly-placed couple of smaller branches, eventually using the nearer of them as a foothold.

It was while he was working out his best approach — which was really his only approach, but Hughie always believed in letting people see that he was thinking about what he was up to — that Tally came along New Walk and stopped to observe what was going on. She had actually been on her way to see Hughie to talk to him about joining The Swimming Club, something that had been bothering her ever since their first visit to Rule Street Baths almost a week ago. She wanted to know whether Hughie, too, felt that he was being used by Jay simply to make some pocket money. Now, though, she was gripped by the scene high above her head. It seemed to her that Hughie was taking a precarious route.

Hughie took another step, a tentative one this time. He was confident the branch would continue to bear his weight; but he was less sure that he would be able to reach the chestnuts after all without first climbing higher and then leaning down. He was beginning to wish he'd never agreed to help Nic and Matthew; he'd forgotten that he actually volunteered to harvest their desired conkers.

Now he slid his left foot another half metre or so along the branch, leaning over to one side as he did so in order to retain a hold on the supportive branch above his head. If only he could bring his right foot across and then—

"Careful, Hughie! That looks risky," Tally yelled.

Her voice startled him. He'd been completely unaware of her arrival. Automatically, he looked down — lost his balance — and slipped sideways.

"Look out!" Nic yelled, instinctively. Matthew, taking the warning personally, ducked away, determined to avoid being crushed by a falling body. Tally didn't utter a word, but her hands flew to her mouth in horror as she saw what was happening.

Hughie, though, didn't fall. By good fortune he managed to grab hold of the branch he'd been moving along, grabbed it with his free right hand. And it was because he was already clinging on to another branch with his left hand that his body twisted violently to one side . . . which sent an agonizing pain shooting down his side and across the small of his back. It was the worst pain he'd ever known in his life and he couldn't prevent himself crying out. It couldn't have been worse if he'd crashed on to the path, or so he believed at that moment.

"Hughie, are you all right? What's wrong?" Tally called as the young boys simply stared upwards, wide eyed in amazement at their hero's obvious plight.

The pain was beginning to recede a little but it flared up again immediately when Hughie tried to move into a safer position. Again, he gasped. Beads of sweat were now standing out on his forehead.

"I — think — I've — damaged — something," he announced. "I've got this — this terrific pain in my side. Did it — twisting — I think."

Once again, Tally found herself wondering

what action to take where Hughie was concerned. She looked round. This time, however, there was no sign of Jay dashing forth in an attempt to rescue him.

"Look, I'd better call an ambulance or the police or, or somebody," she called up to him, her hands now clasped behind her neck as they usually were when she was agitated. "I'll find—"

"No, no, don't do that!" Hughie yelled. "I'm not a *hospital* case, you know."

Nic and Matthew were perhaps more alarmed than anyone by what was happening. If the police turned up then, they suspected, they'd be in deep trouble for damaging the trees, if nothing else. They were also dismayed to discover that their new hero was so feeble that he was complaining of severe pain when he'd done nothing apart from make a tiny slip. If he'd fallen and broken a leg that would have been different; they could have seen the extent of his injury. Matthew had an idea that it would be best if he and his mate just disappeared; after all, Hughie now had a friend of his own to sort things out. But he didn't think Dominic would agree to that.

Tentatively, Hughie tried another movement. This time the pain wasn't so severe. All the same, he knew he was going to have to twist his body quite considerably in order to reach safety, and that might bring the pain flooding back. He was sure he hadn't broken anything. If he'd snapped a rib or something he would surely have heard it, just as he had heard his wrist break when he'd fallen on it as a seven-year-old. So it was probably a ligament he'd torn. A pulled muscle, he reckoned, wouldn't cause quite so much discomfort. (Luckily he was wrong; it was just that he hadn't damaged a muscle quite so badly before and therefore wasn't aware how painful it could be.)

"Look, you can't get down on your own, can you?" Tally said. "So we'll have to get somebody to help. I'll—"

"Hang about!" Hughie ordered. "I haven't given it a proper go yet. I'm just feeling my way."

He was beginning to transfer some of his annoyance with himself to Tally. Until she'd come along and yelled a stupid remark at him he'd been in no danger at all; he'd been within centimetres of reaching his objective. Now she was going to mess things up again if he didn't stop her.

"Shall I get a ladder, Hughie?" Nic inquired, anxiously. "I mean, I could go to one of those houses over there and ask them to lend us one. I'm sure they would if they knew what we wanted it for."

"Might think you're a burglar!" cracked Hughie, unable to resist witticism even when he was suffering. It was, though, the most sensible suggestion so far and Hughie felt he'd accept the offer if he couldn't get down on his own.

"Burglars don't ask for ladders at the houses they're about to burgle," remarked Tally rather unnecessarily. But then she wished she'd thought of calling for a ladder to help rescue Hughie. She wasn't going to admit it but she felt at least partly responsible for causing his slip.

Very cautiously now, he eased himself back

along the branch, a manoeuvre more difficult than he could ever have imagined because he didn't want to release his hold on the higher branch. One more slip and, he feared, he'd be a goner. The path beneath would be about as soft as concrete. This time the stab of pain wasn't so severe. He unclasped his fingers, backed up another few centimetres, felt for a new foothold, turned his shoulders and—

"Ouch!" he exploded. He couldn't help it. Someone seemed to be driving a hot skewer into his kidneys, or where he supposed his kidneys must be: unimaginable torture . . .

"Don't move, Hughie!" Tally ordered. "I'm going to get help. Otherwise there's going to be a terrible accident."

For once, Hughie did as he was told. Tally turned to look for a phone box and, just then, a tall young man with his hands thrust deep in the pockets of his red-and-blue anorak came strolling by. She ambushed him, explaining exactly what was wrong. His amused gaze took in Hughie's predicament.

"No problem," he announced, glancing round. His first instruction was to Tally and Matthew. "Go to that house over there and ask if they've a ladder I can borrow. I don't need it to get up there but I'll need something to put your mate on if I'm going to get him down."

Tally, resisting the urge to say "I told you!" to Hughie, sped away, thankful that somebody else was now in charge of the rescue operation. Hughie, too, was thankful: the young man with the drooping moustache wasn't anyone he knew and wasn't anyone in uniform. Once more, the pain had subsided. It was beginning to infuriate him that he couldn't get down on his own but he wasn't going to risk aggravating his injury. He had too many sporting highlights to look forward to in the next few weeks, the swimming match with Outlane Otters being one of them. In the past few days Hughie had begun to imagine what it would be like to be the world champion backstroker (or backcrawler as a mate at school called it, a word that Hughie, naturally, didn't consider at all appropriate).

Faced with Tally's plea, which was supported by the dramatic claim that there was "a boy stuck up a tree in great pain" the householder promptly obliged with the loan of his ladder. He also helped Tally and Matthew carry it to the scene of the disaster where Gary, the man with the moustache, had by now worked out precisely how to carry out his rescue operation.

"Just don't move, Hughie lad, and you'll be fine, I promise you," Gary instructed; and Hughie, to his credit, did as he was told. "I'm going to have to, sort of, lift you like a fireman does. But don't let that bother you."

It all looked a bit undignified to those waiting below, but that didn't trouble the victim, who was simply concerned with avoiding further pain. And Gary was so considerate and skilful that Hughie felt scarcely a single twinge, even when he made his own way down the ladder. He even began to suppose that his troubles were over — until, foolishly, he attempted to find out by flexing his back, and the pain flared up again.

"Just take it easy, it'll soon get better," said Gary comfortingly, as Hughie remembered to thank him for the rescue. "At your age I twisted a muscle like that and it was agony. But only for a few days. These things don't last."

"Hope you're right," muttered Hughie, as he headed for home, moving as cautiously as a gouty old man on an ice rink. Matthew and Dominic didn't display much sympathy before they went off with Tally to return the ladder, the householder being quite content to let them carry it back for him. The incident had enlivened his day.

"You should check it out with a doctor, you know," recommended Tally, when she caught up with Hughie. She felt that somebody should accompany him home and, anyway, she still wanted to talk to him about The Club.

"No chance! I'll just put some ice on it if it swells up. Or maybe some strapping. I've a friend who knows about sports injuries and how to deal with 'em. So I'll do what he says and—"

"But it isn't a sports injury, is it?" Tally remarked unwisely, her passion for the truth overcoming her judgment of when to ignore it.

"You're not to tell anyone that!" Hughie retorted, fiercely. "I don't want *anybody*, anybody at all, to know what happened. I'll look a right idiot if they hear I did my back in collecting conkers. They'll think I wanted 'em for myself!"

"But you didn't get the conkers, did you, Hughie?" Matthew scoffed, he and Dominic having raced back to rejoin their ex-hero. Now they were interested to see whether his alleged injury would cause him to collapse before he could reach home.

"Get lost!" Hughie exploded. "Go on, scarper! If it hadn't been for your stupid little boy games this would never have happened."

Momentarily, the younger boys looked stunned. But Hughie's tone was enough to send them on their way. It would be some time before they cast any more admiring glances in Hughie's direction.

"Look, you're not to say anything at The Club, O.K.?" Hughie repeated to Tally when they were on their own again. "Janet's the sort of coach who'd want all the medical details if she knew you'd been injured. Wouldn't let you swim if you're not in peak condition, one hundred per cent, you know."

"Listen, there's something I wanted to talk to you about, the reason why I was coming to see you tonight," Tally said, hoping that their conversation would help him to forget his mishap. Crisply, she related what she had seen and heard when Janet spoke to Jay about the bounty money and how it had worried her. "I mean, it's obvious, isn't it? Jay was just using us to get herself some money. What d'you think?"

Hughie shrugged and then wished he hadn't because the movement affected muscles in his side. "Doesn't bother me, Tally. Don't thinks there's anything wrong in it. Good luck to her."

"But don't you think she's just using us to get something for herself, that she doesn't care whether we're any good as swimmers or not?"

Tally persisted.

"So what? *She* doesn't decide whether we're good or not. That's the coach's decision — and Janet seems to think we're O.K. you and me." He halted and turned to look at her. "I'm glad I've joined The Swimming Club because now I've found out I'm good at something else. And so are you. You were great the way you swam that butterfly against Jay — had her really worried, anyone could see that. So that's all you want to think about."

"But getting money just for introducing new members . . . ."

"What's wrong with that, if the rules say you can do it? Jay must be entitled to a reward if Janet's giving it to her." He paused and then another thought occurred to him. "Anyway, now we are members we can find new swimmers and sign them up and get some bounty money for ourselves! That'd be great."

"Tally knew now she wasn't going to get any support for her view about being exploited. There was no point in going on about it because that would only antagonize Hughie, and she felt she'd already caused him to suffer enough. For the remainder of the short but slow walk to his house she patiently listened to a typical recital of his sporting ambitions at everything from basketball to the backstroke.

Hughie wasn't entirely insensitive to other people's feelings and, when he turned to say goodnight to Tally, he saw how glum she was. He knew the cause. "Look," he told her, "if you think Jay's put one over you or something like that you know what to do to get your own back, don't you?"

"What?" Tally asked, simply in order to say something.

"Beat her in the pool, that's what! Show her you're a better swimmer than she is. That'll really make Jay mad."

"A BIT RAPID"

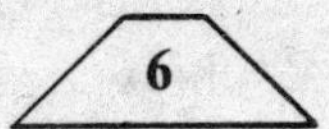

Janet was the one who was mad: mad that Hughie hadn't turned up as promised for the training sessions, and mad with herself for expecting him to be reliable. In the past she'd had proof that boys didn't always keep up their enthusiasms, especially when rigorous training was required before success could be achieved. Often enough, when something easier or more interesting caught their eye, they'd switch to that. Yet she'd convinced herself that Hughie McGavin was different, that he would be one of the future stars of The Swimming Club, that *he* would never let her down.

Her anger was so great that, two days before the match with Outlane Otters was due to take place, the coach turned up on Hughie's front doorstep, demanding to see her missing swimmer. It was a visit that startled Mrs McGavin who initially assumed that this tall, dark-haired young woman with an unmistakable air of authority was one of her son's teachers and that, therefore, he must have committed some dire offence at school. That made her furious, too. And her attitude didn't change even when she learned the truth.

"I'll get him down for you, Miss Gainfield, and you can tell him just what you think of him. If I'd known he was letting you down I'd've given him a rare old talking to myself. But he never let on to me that he was getting involved with proper swimming."

Janet liked that phrase "proper swimming" and thought she'd probably use it herself on an appropriate occasion. Mrs McGavin's support was encouraging. Those parents who took a genuine interest in their children's leisure-time activities could be very helpful to a swimming coach.

Hughie, having bounced downstairs without knowing who his visitor was but expecting it to be one of his mates, was completely taken aback to see Janet — and, particularly, the expression on her face. But it was one of Hughie's great strengths that invariably he made a rapid recovery from any disaster. He realized that, faced with Janet, he would have to tell her the truth, so he decided to make the best of it. After only the briefest hesitation he launched into a detailed explanation of his misfortune in the horse chestnut tree and the manner in which his "badly pulled muscle" had affected his school life, his social life and, inevitably, his sporting life. It was a quietly tragic tale, quite well told really, as

Janet admitted (but only silently, to herself).

"But you could have warned me that you were not fit to train, that you might not be able to swim against Outlane," Janet told him, with no reduction in the severity of her expression.

"Well, I was going to, Miss — er, Janet — but, well, I — I . . . ." Words failed him. "I'm sorry."

It was the apology that saved him, though he never knew it. "But you're fit now, I take it? You must be from the way you seemed to dash down the stairs."

Hughie really didn't know whether to wince or put on an act of bravado. His injury hadn't caused him any discomfort for a couple of days so it appeared that the strapping his friend had put on for him had been effective; and, of course, he'd been careful about not over-exercising himself. On the other hand, he supposed it could flare up again at any moment if . . . .

"Of course he's all right!" Mrs McGavin declared, forthrightly. "He was leaping about, practising his basketball, not half-an-hour ago. If that doesn't show that he's fit I don't know what does!"

Hughie sighed and Janet's cool grey eyes narrowed. He knew he'd been caught out and she experienced a sense of relief that she certainly wasn't going to share with him.

"Well, in that case I want to see you in that pool, swimming your heart out against Outlane," the coach said, forcefully. "You won't be at peak fitness, I don't suppose, and you'll be short of practice. But you could still get a good result for us."

She paused as if allowing Hughie an opportunity to say something; but he didn't. "I believe you have a lot of ability and I don't want to see it wasted," she continued. "That's why I took the trouble to come round to your house tonight. I can tell you, I don't make a habit of chasing after stray sheep. I usually let them go their own way."

Mrs McGavin was just as impressed as Hughie was by this evidence of Janet Gainfield's belief in his potential as a swimmer. So when he gave the coach a firm promise that he would turn up for a vital practice session the following evening and then turn out against Outlane she had the last word.

"I'll make sure he gets there, Miss Gainfield, even if I have to drag him all the way by his ears!"

"She went to his *home*?" Jay exclaimed in amazement when she heard the news, which didn't take long to get out, and was relayed to her by Kerry who'd picked it up in a casual conversation with Martin Moller at the school they both attended. "Janet would never come round to our house — or yours. She wouldn't visit a girl! She's softer with boys, you know that."

Kerry nodded because she usually did agree with Jay. But when she thought about it she came to the same conclusion. The Swimming Club's coach could often be very strict with her girls, almost as if she disliked them or simply didn't trust them in some way. On the other hand, Janet's praise for a girl who achieved success against the odds could be quite lavish, especially if that success brought glory to The Club.

When Tally turned up at the baths on the evening of the match against Outlane she was able to provide a fuller, and quite amusing, version of Hughie's injury and how it was incurred while collecting conkers. She thought it would do him good for people to know the truth and, suddenly, she was popular with Jay and Kerry and a couple of other girls who hung on every word. But even that topic of conversation couldn't outlast the appearance of the Outlane squad in their spectacular blue-and-white striped swimsuits.

"Hey, they look pretty good, don't they — sort of *professional*," Kerry exclaimed, as their opponents marched out in pairs from their changing area to the sound of stirring music on the public address system. "Now why didn't Janet think of getting identical suits for us? I mean, it's O.K. having our name on tracksuit tops but that doesn't make us a team, does it?"

"Oh, I think we should stick to what we want to wear," Jay retorted. "At least we are individuals. That's what counts."

Kerry had spotted something else. "Hey, who's that tiny kid — Chinese or something, is she? Honestly, she looks as if she's hardly big enough for primary school yet!"

Lucie Fortunoff, whose own figure could scarcely have been in greater contrast, had the answer. "She's called Jinko — yeah, her *real* name, weird though it may sound — and she's Japanese. Her father's over here working in that

factory near our school — electronics or something weird like that. Actually, I have swum against her and she's, well, a bit rapid." "Rapid" was the in word at The Club and it was always an understatement.

"She's not in the butterfly, is she?" asked Tally, who was again on the edge of the group.

But before anyone could reply, Janet strode up, demanding why they weren't already changed and ready to swim for their very lives — one of her favourite phrases.

Janet wasn't just nervous about the outcome of the match, she was angry with herself for not having guessed that Outlane would turn up in matching outfits. A ploy like that was typical of

Claire, their coach, who would want her swimmers to exude confidence and an air of superiority. Claire, she realized, was just as competitive in everything she did as Janet herself. However, Outlane wouldn't become better swimmers just by wearing special clothes: as long as The Club's team was in top form they would surely defeat their rivals, or so Janet believed.

Outlane, inevitably, had brought plenty of supporters with them and the noise they made as their swimmers paraded around the pool was almost as deafening as the final stages of the race. Kerry, who'd been persuaded to miss the hairdressing demonstration at the Cavendish to turn out for The Club, scanned the rows of spectators, hoping to catch sight of any of the regional selectors Janet had told them might well be present. "If you can catch the eye of one of them with an outstanding performance against Outlane, Kerry, then you could soon be going off on the sort of travels you fancy — as a swimmer," the coach had told her, having discovered how desperately keen the blonde-haired girl was to visit exciting cities and countries. That remark had been a revelation to Kerry because it had never seriously occurred to her that she could achieve her ambition through swimming, in spite of all Jay's comments on the subject in the past. Until then Kerry hadn't realized how much Janet thought of her abilities in the water.

"Couldn't see anyone interesting — you know, anyone who might pick us for a top swim," Kerry remarked to Jay as they changed together before their first event, the two-lengths butterfly. It wasn't really the best thing to have said: Jay was already in a sombre mood, brooding about the threat to her supremacy from Tally. In the past week Tally had been training with demonic energy and determination.

"Want me to fix your hair before we go out?" she inquired when there was no response. There really wasn't much more she could do to Jay's short, highlighted style but it would give her something to do, and attending to someone's hair always calmed her nerves.

"I'm wearing this," replied Jay, producing to Kerry's astonishment, a vivid black-and-yellow cap from her sports bag. "Could help cut down drag, you know — bit sleeker than my head."

Kerry might have cracked a joke about that until she sensed that her best friend was deadly serious. Sometimes Jay had the capacity to amaze people with her attitudes. "Well, everyone will definitely be able to spot you," she said instead.

"That's the idea," Jay responded, coolly.

Kerry, who had her own long hair tied up and hated to have it covered by anything, just raised an eyebrow. By the time they reached the pool the din was tremendous for the first event was in progress, a three-lengths medley for the younger members. Outlane's supporters, and their senior swimmers, were cheering on their competitors and one boy was even rushing from one end of the pool to the other to shout instructions and offer encouragement.

"Honestly, you'd think this was the Olympics they're competing in," remarked Jay, disapprovingly.

"No, they wouldn't get away with that sort of thing there," Kerry replied. She took a seat on a bench and watched the event reach its climax. In the very last metre of the race an Outlane swimmer drew ahead to win by a fingertip.

"Fantastic! Great result, Emillimetre!" yelled a spectator sitting close to Jay and Kerry. "You've done it again."

Jay and her best friend exchanged amazed glances. They thought the girl sounded hysterical but couldn't resist questioning her.

"Oh, she always does that; wins by a couple of millimetres or something like that," was the reply. "Uncanny, really, how she judges it. But she seems to. Oh yes, and her name is Emily, of course. Actually, she used to hate being called Emillimetre but now she definitely likes it."

After that inspiring start the Outlane team appeared to be in unbeatable form. Only Heidi, in the two-lengths breastroke, recorded a victory for The Swimming Club in the first six events. Janet's gloom was deepening visibly by the minute and most of her team were anxious to keep out of her way when they weren't competing. Only Hughie seemed unaffected by what was going on. Now that he was more or less back in favour — well, the coach said she'd forgiven him — and he was shortly to be back in action he was quite cheerful. It didn't take him long to discover who his likeliest rivals were in the Outlane squad, so he was able to indulge in all his usual boasting about how nobody would be able to catch him. If he could cause opponents to worry about him before any of them were even in the water then surely he'd gained what could be a crucial advantage over them. That was his thinking, anyway.

Janet didn't see it quite like that. On her way to deliver final instructions to her butterfly girls she paused for a word with the boy she regarded as the certain winner of the backstroke race.

"It doesn't help to get too friendly with the opposition," she told him, severely. "Quite the reverse, in fact: it takes the cutting edge off your attack. Makes you less keen to slaughter the enemy. Understand?"

"Er, yes, Mis — er, Janet. Sorry."

"Right. So if you want to chat people up start on our team. Instil some *confidence* in them."

Hughie nodded. But by then Janet was briskly bearing down on the three girls who were representing The Club in the next event: Jay, Kerry and Tally. She favoured Jay as the winner — though she suspected that Tally, the new girl with great potential, might keep up with her. Then there was Kerry, who had always been beaten by Jay in the butterfly up till now. But Kerry was a wonderful swimmer, and of course if she consented to do her best . . .

"Like your cap, Jay," she said, with nods of approval. "Looks aggressive. And that's good. We need somebody to get in there and lead the way. Don't know what's up with our team tonight."

Nobody dared comment that it did seem as if Outlane had the stronger all-round swimmers; they were plainly more experienced than The Club's. Janet, though, would never concede superiority to others.

Now her cool eyes were assessing them all. "Feel good do you? Feel like *swamping* that lot?" Nods were what she got in return: some vigorous, some half hearted. Nerves were beginning to play their part in the preliminaries.

Beaming more broadly than ever, Claire Sanders bounced up to them as her own three girls mounted the starting blocks. But before she could say anything Janet indicated the pencil-slim Japanese girl who was going to be in the fourth lane.

"Are you sure she's the right age for this event?" she interrogated her rival coach. "Looks much too young to me. I mean, we don't want any disputes about qualifications, do we?"

Claire's smile didn't dim by so much as a single watt. "Oh, she's old enough all right; just hasn't filled out yet. But if you doubt me I can show you a photostat of her birth certificate. Always carry one around for every swimmer — saves any arguments developing. Don't you do that, Janet?"

Janet's frown deepened. For the first time as long as she could remember she felt she was being outwitted.

"No, no, of course not! Never found anything like that necessary. I mean, I'm always willing to accept the word of a colleague."

"Good!" responded Claire, in a tone that showed the utmost satisfaction.

The starter was already into his litany and the sextet of swimmers were seconds away from hitting the water.

"Well, may the best girl win," murmured Janet, as if to ease the tension.

Claire's reply was as jovial as the previous one. "Oh, my girl will do that all right. No doubt whatsoever."

THE REAL RACE

By a margin that was barely measurable, Jay was the first into the pool. Kerry, who'd been close to anticipating the starting signal and only just rocked back on to her feet in time, was actually the last, to her own great annoyance. Now that her eagerness to compete had returned she wanted to lead all the way, even in the butterfly. She wanted Jay to chase *her* from now on.

Tally, who'd been practising her turns daily in secret with the aim of making a shallower glide for a more rapid return to the surface, was content to settle in third place for the present. Ahead of her was the little Japanese swimmer, her black pony tail sometimes bobbing above the water line like a periscope. The other two Outlane competitors were in fourth and fifth positions. They knew what Janet and The Swimming Club would never have suspected: that they were taking part simply to make up a team. Neither of them had the remotest hope of winning this event.

Jay's distinctive, wasp-coloured cap was already serving her purpose. It was attracting the attention of every spectator with the result that supporters of both teams began to yell their support. The noise built up deafeningly.

"Jinko!" — "Jay!" — "Jinko!" It was almost as if no one else counted, as if the race were between the girls now in the first two places, as if the entire outcome of the match depended on who won the girls' two-lengths butterfly, which, with Outlane already leading so comfortably, was of course absurd. But that was how the atmosphere was building up as Jay swooped towards the halfway point.

Kerry was in lane six, which she regarded as something of an insult. But at least she was able to see clearly what was going on in all the other lanes without having to turn her head. Her poor start wasn't even a memory now as she made decisive progress, easily overtaking the two Outlane swimmers trailing behind Tally. Soon, she was sure, she'd overhaul her, too. Tally was moving confidently enough but not gaining at all on the leading pair. For the moment neither Kerry nor Tally was at all worried about her own prospects. But then, on this first length, they'd seen nothing to worry them. Like many swimmers, they assumed the real race would take place in the final half length. So as long as they were in touch at that stage . . .

Flipping neatly through her turn as the outright leader, Jay was intent on increasing her advantage. She'd feared that Kerry might be challenging her at this stage and, although she had always beaten Kerry at the butterfly before, she had great respect for her best friend's ability — when she wanted to use it. But of Kerry there was no sign. She was aware that her Japanese rival was in second place with Tally almost level with her, but Jay still didn't see either of them as a real threat. Tally had shaken her that day in the pool but she couldn't have improved much since then.

It took only about ten seconds for that notion to be proved totally wrong, for, with a quite astonishing surge, Jinko went past Jay and into the lead. To some onlookers who'd never seen Jinko in action before it almost appeared as if Jay had stopped swimming — or that Jinko had discovered a higher gear, an extra source of power. Her rhythm, her timing, her propulsion:

everything was right. She didn't just move ahead — she remorselessly drew clear of everyone.

"Hey!" exclaimed Hughie, fascinated by what he was seeing. "She's as thin as an eel, that kid. So where's she get all that power from?"

Nobody answered because nobody knew.

Janet was too flabbergasted to say anything. Claire Sanders grinned to herself.

The Outlane coach was seeing exactly what she'd hoped, and expected, to see. Janet still found it difficult to believe her eyes. Her professionalism, however, took over and she joined in the applause as Jinko touched home far ahead of the second girl.

But it wasn't Jay in the runner-up's position. Jinko's spectacular performance had unnerved her. In trying to keep pace with the Japanese girl's powerboat-like progress Jay lost her own rhythm completely. If she'd been capable of using one of her own favourite expressions at that moment she'd have said she "drifted off". Kerry, who was by then swimming quite beautifully, and had already overtaken Tally, went clear in second place. She was quite exhilarated by her own achievement and grinned hugely at everyone as she completed her race. Her competitive urge had suddenly resurfaced — which was some sort of consolation prize for Janet Gainfield.

"Told you what'd happen, didn't I?" the Outlane coach couldn't help exulting as she turned to her opposite number just as Jay and Tally dead-heated for third place. "She is a champion, is Jinko. Well, you can see that for yourself, can't you? Oh, and she lives near you,

you know. So, she could easily have joined you instead of us."

"Still time for that," Janet muttered. But she made sure the remark was inaudible to Claire. Then she hurried across to commiserate with her trio of butterflyers. Kerry, naturally, seemed quite pleased with herself but Jay looked shell shocked.

"Could've been a fluke, you know," Janet told her; but when they both glanced at the serene-looking Jinko they knew this result was as true as could be.

"Sorry, Janet," Tally said. "Thought I'd do better than that. I mean—"

"Don't worry, Tally," said the coach, putting an arm round her damp shoulders, "you will next time. I guarantee it."

There was no time to say more to any of them, although she desperately wanted to console Jay who might take an age to get over this defeat. Instead she had to have words with Hughie whose power and breathing skills ought to bring The Swimming Club the sort of victory it desperately needed. Or did Outlane possess another prospective champion in the boys' backstroke?

Hughie had marvelled at Jinko's victory but it in no way undermined his belief in what he was going to do to his opponents. He hadn't a single worry, either, about his fitness. He felt wonderfully well, the wrenched muscle a thing of the past. Because he'd never swum in a match before he was looking forward to his success: Hughie was well aware that he was often at his best the first time he ever tried something out and he was sure it would be just the same tonight.

"I'm relying on you, you know, Hughie," Janet said, coming up to ruffle his spiky hair, a gesture he thoroughly disliked. "Don't let us down, will you?"

"I won't, Miss," he replied instinctively. He still found it confusing to try and treat her as a friend, as she wished her Club members to do. To Hughie, it seemed that she always acted and spoke like a teacher at school, and you had to be polite to everyone on the staff there even if informality was encouraged now and then.

"I think your hair's growing longer by the minute," she went on in a reflective manner. "If you cut it all off, shaved your head completely, you know, you'd probably go faster. Lots of world class swimmers have done that to cut — shave — extra parts of a second off their best times."

Hughie's eyes widened in delight. "Hey, great idea! That'd show everyone I was top class, wouldn't it? Got a razor, Miss — Janet?"

She was able to laugh for the first time since the Outlane squad had arrived at the pool. "Better not, Hughie! We can't have everyone knowing what a trickster you are, can we?"

"Don't mind, Miss. I mean—"

"Look, have you been practising the breathing rhythm I showed you? That's the sort of thing that'll really improve your performance, Hughie. When the arm movement and the breathing are in sync, you can't go wrong."

"Yeah — works like a dream now."

"Good. So my confidence about this result

should match yours." She avoided his hair this time and patted him on the back. "Best of luck then, Hughie."

As they all lined up for their names to be announced Hughie studied his rivals. He wasn't impressed by what he saw. Although it was impossible to tell from a person's physical appearance how well anyone might swim — Jinko had already proved that point — Hughie decided that a fair-haired boy carrying rather a lot of extra weight was the one he'd have to beat. He looked quite cool and assured and he returned Hughie's stare without lowering his eyes.

Martin Moller was also swimming for The Club in this event. One of the very brightest pupils at his school, Martin hadn't yet achieved much success in the water or on the sports field but he was a dogged, determined competitor. Hughie reckoned that Martin might even finish second in this race — to himself, naturally. That would certainly give Janet something to cheer about.

As they slipped into the water Hughie, in lane four, yelled across to Martin in lane two, "You and me'll be first and second, no danger! Me first, you second!" He drew a frown and a wagged finger from the starter but nothing was said. Hughie grinned. He was sure he'd now planted the idea of their defeat in the minds of all their rivals. It didn't occur to him that such a boast might have the opposite effect and spur them on to greater endeavours.

Sim, the boy he'd guessed would be his only challenger from the Outlane team, tightened his

lips and tensed, eager to be the fastest away. But as the gun cracked it was Hughie, inevitably, who shot into the lead like a bolt from a crossbow.

Of course, as he was out of sight no one could really tell that he was already well ahead. And it was that lengthy disappearing act that alarmed Claire Sanders — alarmed her so much that she grabbed hold of an official and insisted the race be stopped. Any possibility that a disaster had occurred had to be investigated immediately. The starter released the rope suspended above the pool at the midway point. When that dropped into the water ahead of them competitors knew their race had been halted for some reason.

"What the hell d'you think you're doing?" Janet demanded furiously, dashing across to Claire and the starter who were peering anxiously into the pool to locate Hughie.

"What's wrong with him? He's not got cramp has he?" Claire asked with what sounded like genuine concern. "I mean—"

She broke off as Hughie resurfaced. Almost at once he tangled with the rope. Shaking the water out of his eyes — he refused to wear goggles — and then seeing the consternation on the faces of some of the spectators he realized what had happened. Now he was as angry as his coach.

"This is just another rotten trick on your part, Claire Sanders," Janet fulminated. "But you're not going to stop my best swimmer like that. Come on, Starter, let's get this race going again. I'm warning you, Claire. I'm going to put in an official protest after all this is over!"

"But I was only doing it for *his* sake," the Outlane coach protested. "I mean, I didn't have any idea he could stay submerged as long as that. He could have been drowning for all I knew."

It was impossible for anyone to judge whether Claire was telling the truth or just finding a plausible way of covering up her cunning; Janet, naturally, knew the truth. The starter, however, was prepared to give Claire the benefit of any doubt.

"Quite right," he nodded approvingly. "Can't take any chances where young lives are at risk.

Anyway, no harm's been done."

Janet wasn't ready to concede that yet. For all she knew, Hughie might now lose his nerve or his rhythm or anything; but not, she prayed, the race.

The swimmers treated the incident as nothing more than a bit of a joke. The poolside squabble between the coaches didn't affect them, either, though that, too, amused them. Hughie, however, had gained something positive. He'd heard Janet describe him as her best swimmer, and now he was eager to win his race by the biggest margin

possible.

None of his rivals had realized just how well he was doing when the race was halted and so they didn't feel overawed as they lined up for the re-start. Sim, too, had heard Janet's comment but it didn't mean anything to him because he was used to coaches exaggerating the talents of squad members. That was all part of the "psychological warfare", as Miss Sanders once expressed it, that existed in competitive swimming.

This time Hughie's bow-like reaction to the sound of the starting pistol carried him to an even longer initial lead. When, at last, his head and arms broke the surface there were gasps from Outlane spectators — and huge cheers from his own Club members. Janet turned triumphantly towards Claire, but Claire avoided her eye. The Outlane coach appeared nonplussed; or sickened; or both. Already she knew that the competent Sim would be no match for the backstroker of this calibre.

And so it proved. Hughie led from start to finish, faltering only on the turn when over eagerness caused clumsiness. It wasn't even certain that he'd touched but Claire wasn't going to risk Janet's ire again by questioning the validity of the turn. After all it wasn't going to make the slightest difference to the result.

Most of The Swimming Club competitors, including Jay, Kerry and Tally, were on their feet cheering him on. It was the first time that night they'd had something to shout about, apart from Heidi's popular victory. So Hughie stormed home, lengths ahead of everyone else. And to his own, and Janet's, delight Martin snatched second place practically in the last split second.

The coach was no longer concerned in the slightest about the overall result of this match with Outlane. In any case, it was only a friendly fixture. Her thoughts were now on much, much higher matters.

"You know what you've done, don't you?" she asked her new hero as she gave him a celebratory hug. But she supplied the answer herself. "You've really put The Swimming Club on the map! Great stuff, Hughie."

Jay overheard that. She bit her lip and then said fiercely, half to herself, "But I'll be the one to keep it there!"

Tally, who was listening to everything, nodded. "Me, too," she said. But no one heard her words. Hughie, adoring all the attention he was getting, had raised his hands above his head and was applauding himself.

Read what happens next to the kids in The Swimming Club in Book 2: JUMP IN.

HAUNTINGS by Hippo Books is a new series of excellent ghost stories for older readers.

Ghost Abbey by Robert Westall
When Maggie and her family move into a run-down old abbey, they begin to notice some very strange things going on in the rambling old building. Is there any truth in the rumour that the abbey is haunted?

Don't Go Near the Water by Carolyn Sloan
Brendan knew instinctively that he shouldn't go near Blackwater Lake. Especially that summer, when the water level was so low. But what was the dark secret that lurked in the depths of the lake?

Voices by Joan Aiken
Julia had been told by people in the village that Harkin House was haunted. And ever since moving in to the house for the summer, she'd been troubled by violent dreams. What had happened in the old house's turbulent past?

The Nightmare Man by Tessa Krailing
Alex first sees the man of his darkest dreams at Stackfield Pond. And soon afterwards he and his family move in to the old house near the pond — End House — and the nightmare man becomes more than just a dream.

A Wish at the Baby's Grave by Angela Bull
Desperate for some money, Cathy makes a wish for some at the baby's grave in the local cemetery. Straight afterwards, she finds a job at an old bakery. But there's something very strange about the bakery and the two Germans who work there. . .

The Bone-Dog by Susan Price
Susan can hardly believe her eyes when her uncle Bryan makes her a pet out of an old fox-fur, a bone and some drops of blood — and then brings it to life. It's wonderful to have a pet which follows her every command — until the bone-dog starts to obey even her unconscious thoughts. . .

All on a Winter's Day by Lisa Taylor
Lucy and Hugh wake up suddenly one wintry morning to find everything's changed — their mother's disappeared, the house is different, and there are two ghostly children and their evil-looking aunt in the house. What has happened?

The Old Man on a Horse by Robert Westall
Tobias couldn't understand what was happening. His parents and little sister had gone to Stonehenge with the hippies, and his father was arrested. Then his mother disappeared. But while sheltering with his sister in a barn, he finds a statue of an old man on a horse, and Tobias and Greta find themselves transported to the time of the Civil War. . .

Look out for these forthcoming titles in the HAUNTING series:
The Rain Ghost by Garry Kilworth
The Haunting of Sophy Bartholomew by Elizabeth Lindsay

THE MALL

Six teenagers, all from different backgrounds, with one thing in common – they all want jobs at the new shopping Mall opening in Monk's Way. But working at the Mall brings rather more than most of them had bargained for . . .

Book 1: **Setting Up Shop**

Book 2: **Open for Business**

The new shopping Mall is opening soon, and the six teenagers who work there are already having problems. Ian is fired from his job at Harmony Records because of his dad's interference. Amanda's trying to fend of Mr Grozzi's advances at the restaurant. Jake's trying to hold down two jobs at once. And Simon's temper is threatening to cost him his job at the furniture store. Will life at the Mall prove too tough to handle?.

Look out for the next books in The Mall series:

Book 3: **Gangs, Ghosts and Gypsies**
Book 4: **Money Matters**

You'll find these and many more fun Hippo books at your local bookseller, or you can order them direct. Just send off to *Customer Services, Hippo Books, Westfield Road, Southam, Leamington Spa, Warwickshire CV33 0JH*, not forgetting to enclose a cheque or postal order for the price of the book(s) plus 30p for postage and packing.

SAMANTHA SLADE

Samantha Slade's an ordinary girl living in an ordinary town; but when she starts a job out of school babysitting for the Brown children, her uneventful life is turned upside down. Because when Dr Brown tells Samantha her children are little monsters, poor Sam doesn't realize that they really *are* monsters! Lupi turns into a werewolf when the moon is full, and Drake sprouts fangs, drinks tomato ketchup by the crateful and concocts the most amazing potions in his laboratory!

Book 1: **Monster-Sitter**
When Samantha Slade agrees to let Lupi and Drake Brown, the two children she babysits, help her with the school Halloween party, she finds she's created the most realistic haunted house ever! Lupi turns into a real werewolf, the fake creepie crawlies become alive, and the whole thing turns into a riot of terrified kids . . .

Book 2: **Confessions of a Teenage Frog**
Samantha Slade should have known better than to accept help from Lupi and Drake when she's campaigning to become class president. Drake makes her a "greatness potion", and before she knows it, she's been turned into a frog! Will Drake be able to turn her back again before she has to make her big speech for the campaign?

Other titles in the SAMANTHA SLADE series:
Book 3 **Our Friend, Public Nuisance No 1**
Book 4 **The Terrors of Rock and Roll**

THE STEPSISTERS
When Paige's Dad marries Virginia Guthrie from Atlanta, she's thrilled that he's found someone to make him happy. But how will she get on with her new stepbrother and stepsisters? Especially Katie, the beautiful blonde fifteen-year-old, who looks like a model and can charm her way out of anything!

1 The War Between the Sisters £1.75
Not only does Paige have to share her room with her stepsister, Katie, but then she finds that Jake, the boy she's fallen in love with, finds Katie totally irresisitible. Paige's jealousy leads her to do some pretty stupid things to get her own back . . .

2 The Sister Trap £1.75
Paige is delighted when she gets a job working on the school magazine. Especially when she becomes friendly with the magazine editor, Ben. But her jealousies over her beautiful stepsister, Katie, flare up again when Ben starts taking a lot of interest in Katie's swimming career.

Look out for these new titles in
THE STEPSISTERS series:
3 Bad Sisters
4 Sisters in Charge

You will find these and many more great Hippo books at your local bookseller, or you can order them direct. Just send off to *Customer Services, Hippo Books, Westfield Road, Southam, Leamington Spa, Warwickshire CV33 0JH*, not forgetting to enclose a cheque or postal order for the price of the book(s) plus 30p per book for postage and packing.